Savannah, Augusta & Brier Creek

About the Author

Daniel McDonald Johnson is a former newspaper reporter. He began his research on the Battle of Brier Creek while serving as associate publisher of *The Telephone* in Sylvania, Georgia, from 1995 to 1997. He now serves as a librarian at the University of South Carolina Salkehatchie.

He is the author of *This Cursed War: Lachlan McIntosh in the American Revolution*, available initially only in hardback. His earlier books are available in paperback and on Kindle.

Blood on the Marsh is a sprawling epic that traces the families who settled Darien, Georgia, from their ancestral home in the Scottish Highlands to the southern frontier of Colonial America, and describes their participation in the Jacobite Risings and the American Revolution. *Blood on the Marsh* also presents the history and legend of Flora MacDonald, who rescued Bonnie Prince Charlie in the Jacobite Rising of 1745, emigrated to the Cross Creek country of North Carolina, remained loyal to Britain during the American Revolution, and returned to Scotland. Another Scots Highlander from the Cross Creek country, Allen McDonald, supported the patriot cause during the American Revolution, and his exploits in the 2nd South Carolina Regiment and in Marion's Brigade are recorded in *Blood on the Marsh*.

A shorter, more focused book titled *Mr. McIntosh's Family* deals with the Mackintosh clan and the McIntosh family in the Jacobite Risings, the settlement of Darien, Georgia, and the struggle for the Colonial American southern frontier.

Savannah, Augusta & Brier Creek

Samuel Elbert and his resistance against the conquest of Georgia

Daniel McDonald Johnson

Copyright © 2018 by Daniel McDonald Johnson
Post Office Box 747
Allendale, South Carolina, 29810
All rights reserved

ISBN-13:
978-0-692-16677-2

CONTENTS

PART ONE: A NARRATIVE HISTORY

1. The Capture of Savannah ---------------- 5
2. The March to Augusta ------------------- 13
3. The Battle of Brier Creek --------------- 21
4. Afterword -------------------------------- 31

PART TWO: LEGENDS

5. An Accusation of Atrocities -------------- 39
6. Legendary Last-second Rescues -------- 47
7. The Legend of Cannon Lake -------------- 51
8. The Adventures of John McIntosh------ 53
9. Bodies in Motion --------------------------- 61
10. Reflections of Legends ------------------- 65

PART THREE: A BIOGRAPHY

11. Samuel Elbert ------------------------------ 73

(Continued on next page)

CONTENTS
(Continued)

PART FOUR: REVOLUTIONARY WAR SITES

12. Remember Brier Creek ------------------- 93
13. Come See Us --------------------------------- 99
14. The Brier Creek Battleground--------- 107
15. Paddle to the Battle ----------------------- 115
16. Along the Savannah River ---------------117
    Savannah ------------------ 117
    Purrysburg ---------------- 119
    Ebenezer ------------------- 120
    Two Sisters Ferry -------- 123
    Tuckasee King ------------ 124
    Hudson's Ferry ----------- 125
    Miller Bridge -------------- 126
    Matthews Bluff ----------- 128
    Burton's Ferry ------------ 133
    Paris's Mill ----------------- 134
    Augusta --------------------- 134

Notes --- 139
Bibliography ------------------------------------- 157
Index --- 165

Savannah, Augusta &
Brier Creek

PART ONE

A NARRATIVE HISTORY

Georgia's role in the American Revolution bears the dubious distinction of being the only state conquered by Great Britain and returned to colonial rule. The British captured Savannah late in 1778, occupied Augusta briefly in the first part of 1779, and cemented control of Georgia with a victory at Brier Creek on March 3, 1779.

Chapter 1

The Capture of Savannah, December 1778

SAMUEL ELBERT KNEW how to defend Georgia. He had studied military science in England, he had formed a colonial militia company, and he had led Continental troops in Georgia since the beginning of the American Revolution.[1]

When Lieutenant Colonel Archibald Campbell led a British expedition to Georgia in December of 1778, Elbert knew Georgia faced a terrible threat, and he knew the best way to defend against it. He knew that Brewton's Hill plantation on the Savannah River offered the only feasible landing place for the British invaders intent on capturing Savannah, and he knew the British invasion could be stopped if the American army took a defensive position on the bluff rising forty feet above the landing. But Elbert was not in command of the American army. Although Elbert commanded the Georgia Continental regiments, Major General Robert Howe, a North Carolinian who had remained in Savannah after being replaced as commander of the Southern Department headquartered in Charleston, held overall command over American forces in Georgia. Elbert advised Howe that the bluff at Brewton's Hill "should be fortified and defended to the last extremity." Howe failed to heed Elbert's advice and placed only forty men at Brewton's Hill.[2]

ARCHIBALD CAMPBELL DESERVED to be a general in the British army. He had been assigned to lead eight battalions in an invasion of Georgia for the purpose of reestablishing British rule over the rebellious colony. He expected to be promoted from lieutenant colonel to brigadier general "to add weight and consequence to the trust reposed in me," but other officers objected on the basis of seniority. "Although I felt myself greatly disappointed in not obtaining the rank promised me," he wrote in a journal for publication, "yet the reflection of commanding three thousand men and of having an opportunity in exerting myself in the service of my king and country overbalanced every other consideration."[3]

In a letter not intended for publication, Campbell let his bitterness show. "I was obliged to march at the head of three thousand men as a lieutenant colonel in a country where lieutenant colonels and cobblers spring up like mushrooms, and are equally respected," Campbell complained to a friend. A colonel's name on a proclamation, Campbell wrote, "would have no other weight with the populace but what my arms enforced."[4]

CAMPBELL HAD COMPILED a distinguished record of service to his king and country. Before his nineteenth birthday he had been appointed an ensign in the Corps of Engineers. He rapidly rose to the rank of captain-lieutenant and served in the West Indies. By his twenty-ninth birthday he held the rank of lieutenant colonel and served as chief engineer in Bengal for more than four years. After a brief stint with the East India Company, he served as a lieutenant colonel in the East Indies.

He returned to Scotland and took a seat in Parliament in 1774 that he continued to hold while he served in the American war. In 1775 he helped raise the 2nd Battalion of the 71st Regiment, often called the Highlanders because the soldiers were recruited in the Highlands of Scotland. The regiment sailed from Scotland to reinforce the British forces in Boston. By the time the fleet reached America, Boston had been seized by the American rebels. Campbell was on one of the British transport ships that sailed into Boston Harbor and was captured by the Americans. Eventually, in May of 1778, Campbell was released in a prisoner exchange for Ethan Allen. Because Campbell missed the first two years of the American Revolution while he was a prisoner of war, his first opportunity to serve his king and country during the war came when he was appointed to subdue Georgia.

A FLEET of at least twenty warships and troop transports set sail on November 26, 1778, to carry Campbell's army from New York to the coast of Georgia. On December 23, the fleet came to anchor off Ossabaw Island, about twenty miles from the mouth of the Savannah River. The next day the fleet entered the river. Campbell sent scouts on two flatboats up the river to find a landing place for his troops. The scouts reported that the only suitable landing place was at Brewton's Hill, a plantation belonging to John Girardeau. "From this intelligence I proposed," Campbell wrote in his journal entry for December 26, "I should push on shore in the middle of the night at Girardeau's plantation with one thousand men, and establish a footing before daylight." His plan was foiled when "the night proved so boisterous, and the wind so contrary, it was impossible to execute this service."[5]

When the weather eventually calmed, Campbell personally led the attack on forty Americans guarding the bluff at Brewton's Hill. "On this bluff a small body of rebels appeared in readiness for our reception," Campbell reported, "having occupied the houses and barns of the plantation and knocked out planks for their firelocks to look through."

A narrow bank with deep ditches on each side crossed a soggy rice field that lay between the landing place and the bluff. The bank was so narrow that only two soldiers could march side by side as they crossed. At dawn on December 29, 1778, a corporal and four Highlanders from the 71st Regiment set out across the bank followed by a sergeant and twelve Highlanders about fifty yards back, followed by Campbell and a light infantry company of Highlanders. Altogether, five hundred British soldiers had landed. When the British approached within one hundred yards of the American position, the Americans opened fire. Campbell launched his company of light infantry in a Highland charge toward the Americans. The Highlanders "rushed on with such rapidity that in less than three minutes we were in possession" of the bluff at Brewton's Hill, Campbell reported. "The rebels retreated with precipitation by the back doors and windows" of John Girardeau's house and barns. "This acquisition was a favorable presage of our future success and were it not for the loss of Captain Cameron, an officer of distinguished merit and bravery, who with three Highlanders were killed, and five Highlanders wounded, nothing could have turned out more fortunate."

Campbell confirmed that Samuel Elbert had identified the best way to defend against Campbell's attack. "Had the rebels stationed four pieces of cannon on this bluff with five hundred men for its defense," Campbell observed, "it is more than probable they would have destroyed the greatest part of this division of our little army in their progress to the bluff."

As soon as Campbell took possession of Brewton's Hill and secured the landing place, he sent out scouts who reported that the Americans had taken a defensive possession on the southern edge of the Savannah River. Wanting to attack quickly, Campbell led about two thousand troops into battle while the rest of his troops continued to disembark from the troop transports. When Campbell got within eight hundred yards of the enemy, he climbed a tall tree to study the American defenses. A marshy stream separated the British and American forces. One flank of the American army extended to marshes and rice fields beside the Savannah River. The other flank appeared to be protected by swampland.

Campbell, combining his talents as an engineer and a military tactician, looked for a way to maneuver behind the American lines. A slave from a nearby plantation told Campbell that a path led through the swamp that lay beside the right flank of the American army. Campbell sent about six hundred light infantrymen across the path through the swamp while the main body of his command prepared to assault the center of the American position.[6]

SAMUEL ELBERT MOVED INTO POSITION on the left side of the American line near the Savannah River. He commanded what remained of the Georgia Continental brigade after a series of disastrous expeditions to Florida. The brigade was armed, Elbert said, with a "medley of rifles, old muskets and fowling pieces."[7]

The responsibility for defending Savannah fell on about 650 Continental troops from Georgia and South Carolina, about one hundred Georgia militiamen who were even more poorly equipped than the Continental troops, and a small artillery unit.

When the British light infantry emerged from the swamp and attacked Georgia militia at the military barracks inside Savannah, well behind the American defensive position on the edge of town, General Howe ordered the American defenders to retreat. The South Carolina brigade withdrew first, the artillery unit went next, and Elbert brought the Georgia brigade into position to cover the rear of the retreat. General Howe reported that Elbert's brigade withdrew from the battle line in "perfect good order."

The South Carolina brigade moved quickly enough to escape from town before the British light infantry cut off the line of retreat. Elbert's Georgia brigade fell behind and came under fire from the British light infantry. Another British detachment cut off the line of retreat along the Augusta Road leading out of Savannah to the west. Elbert decided to fight through what he considered a weak stretch of the British line so that his brigade could escape down the Ogeechee Road to the south. Elbert issued orders: "Halt! Sections, to the left face: By files to the right wheel: March." The brigade broke ranks, however, and most of the Georgians fled down the road into Savannah.

Elbert went with his men and continued to look for an escape route. Another officer told Elbert that a makeshift bridge of logs had been built across Musgrove Creek at Yamacraw on the far edge of Savannah. Elbert waved his sword above his head and shouted, "Follow me, soldiers, and I will conduct you to a safe retreat." When the soldiers reached the bank of Musgrove Creek, however, they could not find a bridge. The creek was at high tide, and if there ever was a bridge then it must have been underwater. They had no choice, Elbert told his men, other than to swim across the tide-swollen creek. Most of the men decided not to take the risk. Elbert and a few officers and men did manage to swim to the far shore and escape. The 186 remaining soldiers were trapped at the bank of the creek. When British attackers opened fire on the Americans, a Georgia major who had stayed behind because he could not swim raised a white flag and surrendered to a British lieutenant.[8]

ARCHIBALD CAMPBELL GLOATED over Samuel Elbert's ignominious retreat. Campbell wrote in his journal, "it was flood tide, and such only who could swim effected their escape. Among these, General Robert Howe, Colonels Huger and Elbert were successful, but they left their horses in the mud."[9]

Campbell's well-conceived attack killed eighty-three American defenders, wounded eleven, and took 488 prisoners, while the British lost only seven killed and nineteen wounded. In a single day, Campbell had driven the American forces out of Georgia, seized the American artillery, small arms, shot, gunpowder and other military stores, and occupied Georgia's capital. Campbell bragged that he was the first British officer to tear a stripe and star out of the Continental flag.[10]

WITH SAVANNAH UNDER British control, Campbell visited several small towns and settlements, urging Georgians to return to the fold as British subjects and to enroll in loyalist militia units. In the process, Campbell's simmering resentment over his rank came to a boil. He placed Commodore Hyde Parker's name ahead of his own name on a proclamation offering "the blessings of peace, freedom and protection most graciously tendered by His Majesty to his deluded subjects of America." Campbell wrote in his journal:

> As the name of Hyde Parker is placed in the first signature to this publication, and as it is certain from the instructions given me by His Majesty's Commissioners that neither this officer nor any other had authority to be joined with me in the reestablishment of civil government in Georgia, it is proper I should explain the motives which induced me to admit of his name being affixed to these publications and to precede my own in all such occasions.
>
> This officer had the title of commodore given him by Admiral Gambier, while it was my misfortune to have no distinction of that nature conferred upon me; being a lieutenant colonel only. Knowing well that such a title was become a mere drag among the rebels (cobblers and blacksmiths enjoying the rank in their army) I thought it more for the interest of government that I should sacrifice my own feelings on this occasion to the public good. Under the impression of such ideas, I entreated of Sir Hyde Parker to suffer me to use his name as the most effectual means of giving greater weight to these publications. Why the temporary rank of brigadier general was refused to a lieutenant colonel of four years standing, who had been selected as a fit officer to be entrusted with the command of eight battalions of infantry on a service of the first importance to the nation, especially as that extra rank could not interfere with or injure any superior officer in the line, is a question that can only be solved by those who had the power of granting it. If at a critical period of the war the punctilios of rank are to be

considered of more essential consequence than the success of His Majesty's army, a superior officer however ill qualified might have been appointed to command the expedition to Georgia.[11]

Campbell's sensitivity to rank soon came up again when a higher-ranking British officer arrived in Savannah. General Augustine Prevost left East Florida and marched up the Georgia coast, capturing the fortified port of Sunbury. As Prevost approached Savannah, Campbell moved out of the best house in town to let Prevost move in. General Prevost arrived at Savannah in mid-January of 1779 and immediately took command of the army that Campbell had brought to Georgia. "In the midst of my successful career," Campbell wrote, "I felt this supercession severely, but he was my superior in rank and it was my duty to obey."[12]

Campbell told a friend that Prevost, at age fifty-nine, "seems a worthy man, but too old and inactive for this service. He will do in garrison, and I shall gallop with the light troop."[13]

While Prevost commanded the garrison in Savannah, Campbell intended to gallop with the light troop to Augusta.

Chapter 2

The March to Augusta, January-February 1779

AFTER ARCHIBALD CAMPBELL captured Savannah, he made plans to capture Augusta, a town at the fall line of the Savannah River that served as the gateway to the backcountry. Campbell set out in late January of 1779 with about a thousand British and loyalist troops. He planned to link up with additional loyalist units coming from the backcountry and also planned to recruit civilians to form loyalist militia.

On January 25, Campbell sent the light infantry to secure a bridge across Brier Creek. "These troops surprised a body of the enemy," Campbell wrote, "and were in sufficient time to save the bridge, which was actually in flames. Some prisoners fell into our hands on this occasion." Brier Creek, Campbell reported, "is about one hundred feet wide at the bridge, and about eight or ten feet in depth; the current of water is slow, and the bottom muddy." Campbell enrolled several men from the Brier Creek neighborhood into the militia and directed them to "keep within the circle of their respective farms, and to fix upon a place of rendezvous in case of an alarm." He established a post at Brier Creek manned with thirty Carolina loyalists and twenty rifle dragoons. He fortified the post with an abbatis (a defensive structure made of tree trunks and limbs) around houses.

Under Prevost's orders, Campbell reluctantly sent the Florida Rangers under Thomas Brown to attack patriots in Burke County. The patriots defeated the Rangers and wounded Brown.[1]

SAMUEL ELBERT WAS FORCED TO FLEE from Georgia during the British capture of Savannah but he did not abandon Georgia.

Under orders from Southern Department commander Benjamin Lincoln, Elbert traveled up the South Carolina side of the Savannah River with plans take command of 150 Continental troops stationed in Augusta.[2] By the end of January he was in the backcountry of Georgia, joining forces with several other patriot officers.[3]

Campbell reported that Elbert was at Telfair's sawmill, about twenty-four miles away from Campbell's army, on January 28. Campbell set out at four o'clock in the morning to confront Elbert but, by the time Campbell reached Telfair's sawmill, Elbert was no longer there. Campbell sent a spy to "examine General Elbert's situation." As night approached, fifty patriot horsemen pursued the spy close to the lines of Campbell's camp. "By the agility of the spy's horse, he escaped," Campbell reported, "and our dragoons in turn pursued and took two of the rebels, from whom I received confirmation of Colonel Brown's intelligence respecting the junction of General Elbert, Colonels Hammond, Ingram and Fiew; and that the enemy had taken post at Boggy Gut to dispute our progress."[4]

Campbell hoped to attack Elbert's force. When the British reached Boggy Gut shortly after daybreak on January 29, however, they found nothing but traces of the Americans' campfires. By noon, spies and scouts informed Campbell that Elbert intended to oppose the British advance at a deep, swampy ravine called Macbean's Creek. At two hours before midnight, the British light infantry and Florida Rangers started secretly working their way through the dark woods to a bluff overlooking Elbert's camp. At two hours after midnight, the main body of Campbell's troops started advancing toward Elbert's position. At four o'clock in the morning of January 30, Campbell arranged his troops for battle.

At daylight British artillery pounded Elbert's position. Seeing no response, Campbell sent his infantry across the creek. They found pots of beef and pork on fires lighted so recently that the water in the pots was just slightly warm. They also found blankets, muskets and provisions that had been left behind by the Americans. All the evidence showed that Elbert had abandoned his position in a hurry. Elbert had captured two Florida Rangers searching for plunder who told him of Campbell's plan for a surprise attack. Elbert managed to withdraw from Macbean's Creek just half an hour before artillery fire signaled the start of the attack.[5]

Elbert fell back ten miles along the road to Augusta. At Spirit Creek, his force of two hundred men took shelter in a small stockade called Fort Henderson. On January 30 Campbell placed a howitzer and two six-pounder cannons on a piece of high ground three hundred yards from the stockade. British artillery fire smashed into the stockade and struck several American soldiers. The Americans scrambled out the stockade "in a very precipitate manner," Campbell reported, but remained in battle formation near Spirit Creek. Campbell's army crossed the creek, occupied the stockade, and formed for battle with the right flank against the stockade. Elbert led the Americans in a retreat toward Augusta.[6]

Campbell received intelligence that Elbert's command had been reinforced and lay in ambush at a swamp called the Cupboard. When the British cautiously approached the Cupboard on January 31 they found no resistance, indicating that the intelligence was false or that the Americans had withdrawn.[7]

After reaching Augusta, Elbert crossed the Savannah River and joined forces with Andrew Williamson, a South Carolina brigadier general. American records indicated a combined forced of twelve hundred men, but Campbell thought he faced eighteen hundred men.[8]

CAMPBELL'S ARMY continued toward Augusta and entered the town early in the evening of January 31, 1779, without resistance. Campbell occupied Augusta for two weeks. He deployed his troops in defensive positions and strengthened the town's fortifications. During the occupation an event occurred that would soon have drastic repercussions. A marauding band of patriots killed Sergeant Hugh MacAlister of the 71st Regiment while he protected a patriot family from reprisals by local loyalists. Campbell described the event in his journal entry for February 3:

> The enemy appeared to have no disposition to disturb us, otherways than by sending a number of small parties across the Savannah River to plunder the inhabitants... One of these parties shot and cruelly cut with hatchets one of our most valuable light infantry men (named MacAlister) who had been placed as a safeguard at the house of a rebel major, about one mile from camp. This major was a prisoner of war in my possession, and entreated in pressing terms to grant him a safeguard for the protection of his wife and family.
>
> The barbarity which accompanied this murder was disgraceful in the extreme and I was in hopes that the rebels would have afforded me instant and ample redress, as General Williamson disclaimed the act and, it is said, loaded the perpetrators with irons; but instead of punishing them with promptness according to their deserts, he sent them to General Lincoln at Purrysburg, who directed their irons to be struck off, and there the business ended. The British troops, however, were greatly exasperated by this shameful act of injustice; especially the light infantry who had determined to avenge MacAlister's murder on the first favorable occasion.[9]

On February 11 Campbell learned that patriot troops from North Carolina would arrive in the evening to reinforce Elbert and Williamson across the river from Augusta. American officers reported the North Carolinians commanded by General John Ashe numbered from nine hundred to eleven hundred, but Campbell's spies estimated the number at sixteen hundred. Campbell believed that his army of one thousand men faced an American army of 3,800 men. Campbell recognized the risk of remaining in Augusta and on February 14 withdrew toward Savannah. Campbell's army found security in the fortified British post at Hudson's Ferry, forty-eight miles from Savannah. When his troops reached Hudson's Ferry on the evening of February 20, "to my great concern there was no rum to be had, notwithstanding repeated letters sent to the general and commissary that this detachment was without rum for many days," Campbell grumbled. "To the honor of these brave fellows, they bore the want of rum like good soldiers."[10]

Campbell, who planned to return to England after conquering Georgia, turned over command of the troops at Hudson's Ferry to Lieutenant Colonel James Mark Prevost, the younger brother of General Augustine Prevost. Campbell wrote in his journal on February 20:

> At this station I met Lieutenant Colonel Prevost, who informed me that he was in the future to command the advance troops and he should be obliged to me for my opinion and advice respecting the intentions of the rebels, which I gave with pleasure by telling him I was well persuaded, if the enemy were not disturbed, they would advance as far as Briar Creek, in which case they might be easily surprised by sending some of our troops to amuse them in front while the rest proceeded up the Back Road towards the bridge at Paris's Mills and came round upon their rear. As the colonel had never seen that country, I showed him my sketch of these parts and explained in the fullest manner the nature of the ground ly-

ing on each side of the Back Road, and that between the creek and the river.[11]

Leaving Colonel Prevost at Hudson's Ferry, Campbell proceeded downriver to the British post at Ebenezer, where he met with General Augustine Prevost. "I took occasion to mention to the general my ideas regarding the motions of the light troops," Campbell wrote. "The probability of the rebels coming down to Briar Creek, and the facility of getting round into their rear by Paris's Mill. I showed him also my sketch of the country on both sides of Briar Creek, which seemed to give him satisfaction."[12]

When he reached Savannah, Campbell took measures to restore British colonial rule in Georgia. He issued a proclamation for enforcing the laws that governed Georgia in 1775 on the eve of the American Revolution. He restored the civil offices of the British colony and set up a police department for the city of Savannah. At the beginning of his expedition, Campbell had been given a commission as governor of Colonial Georgia and, quite optimistically, as governor of Colonial South Carolina. The plan called for him to be replaced as governor of Georgia by the former colonial governor, James Wright, who had escaped from Savannah when the revolution began. On March 4 Campbell appointed a lieutenant governor pro tempore to serve as the chief civil executive from the time Campbell left Georgia until the time Wright arrived. He chose James Mark Prevost because "being the brother of General Prevost, who was so much attached to his welfare and success that there is not a doubt but harmony and unanimity will take place between the civil and military branches of the government." He sent the commission to Prevost at Hudson's Ferry along with a letter:

> I am happy to have it in my power, before I quit America, to fulfill in great measure the interesting object of

His Majesty's Commissioners by re-establishment of legal government in Georgia.

It gives me at the same time great pleasure to reflect that I have it in my power to entrust the commission of Lieutenant Governor into the hands of an officer in whose abilities I place so high a confidence, and who from his knowledge of the country, the temper and inclination of the people, is well qualified to carry into execution the gracious intentions of our Sovereign.[13]

While Campbell was in Savannah restoring colonial rule to Georgia, James Mark Prevost was following Campbell's suggestion for attacking an American army that had, as Campbell predicted, encamped at the junction of Brier Creek and the Savannah River.

Chapter 3

The Battle of Brier Creek: March 3, 1779

SAMUEL ELBERT WANTED to move the camp at Brier Creek away from Miller Bridge. He had been fighting in the swamps of Georgia and Florida for more than three years and he had developed strong opinions on the requirements for a good camp. In the early years of the war he had ordered an officer "to have particular attention paid to his men, to keep them in as high spirits as possible, by all means to make them encamp on a dry spot of ground, and that together, and to let no time be lost in teaching the men discipline."[1]

While General Ashe attended a council of war at Purrysburg, Elbert and General John Bryant moved the camp to higher ground a mile upstream from Miller Bridge. A light infantry detachment of about two hundred men fit for duty commanded by Lieutenant Colonel Anthony Lytle remained at Miller Bridge.

The site Elbert chose for the main encampment occupied a large farm field near a fork in Brier Creek, providing the troops with a convenient source of water. A vast swamp stretched nearly three miles to the Savannah River on the side of the encampment opposite from Brier Creek. The road to Miller Bridge intersected with the road to Augusta at the camp.[2]

The soldiers in camp could not build defensive works because they did not have entrenching tools. They were not issued ammunition because they did not have cartridge boxes. Supplies were nearly impossible to get because Ashe had posted their supply train eight miles away at Burton's Ferry.

The American army remained at Brier Creek for four days waiting for reinforcements. Ashe complained that only 207 mounted soldiers from South Carolina joined him, and only 150 of them were fit for duty.

The American army contained Elbert's band of about a hundred Georgia Continentals and militia, Bryant's brigade of nine hundred North Carolinians, a four-pound field piece and a pair of two-pound swivels mounted as field pieces.

On the other side of the Savannah River, Major John Grimke's South Carolina artillery and General Rutherford's North Carolina regiment of seven hundred infantry arrived at Matthews Bluff. The American plan called for them to cross the river and march three miles to the camp at Brier Creek. Fifty men began building bridges and clearing a road across the swamp from the Georgia side of the Savannah River to the camp at Brier Creek, but they did not complete the job in time for the American plan to take effect.

NEARLY FOUR HUNDRED BRITISH soldiers of the 1st Battalion of the 71st Regiment took a position across Brier Creek from the Americans on March 2. While the Americans watched that battalion, Colonel James Mark Prevost led a force of nine hundred British soldiers on a fifty-mile march to come around behind the Americans.

The British force on the march included the 2nd Battalion of the 71st Regiment under the command of Colonel John Maitland. About forty men of the 71st formed a dragoon company using cavalry equipment seized in Savannah. Sir James Baird commanded two companies of light infantry. The force also included three companies of elite troops of the 60th Regiment, and fifty men of the Florida Rangers.

The British crossed Brier Creek at Paris's Mill, upstream of the American army. The maneuver trapped the Americans between Brier Creek, the Savannah River and the British force.

JAMES FERGUS KNEW HOW to live to fight another day. A native of Pennsylvania, he volunteered on two occasions to serve in the Pennsylvania militia. When he was twenty years old he served at Staten Island during the fighting at New York, and participated in the Battle of Princeton. After his family moved to South Carolina, he volunteered in the campaign to drive the British out of Georgia. In the early months of 1779, his regiment of about two hundred horsemen set out on a two-hundred-mile journey to Augusta.

"It was a very wet winter, the roads exceedingly deep," Fergus recalled in his pension application. "We had a very uncomfortable march and a tedious time on the road. I think there was eight days on the way the sun never appeared to us; it sometimes rained incessantly, and frequently showery. This I can well remember – all that time, the clothes on my back was not dry, nor had I them off, for we had generally to encamp in the woods and always to take care of our horses."

When Fergus finally reached Augusta, he was told to continue marching to the American camp at the junction of Brier Creek and the Savannah River. "The river was very full by reason of the late rains," Fergus remembered, "the backwater extended up the creek twelve miles at least to where it was fordable from where we lay."[3]

Immediately after reaching Brier Creek, the regiment received orders to conduct reconnaissance around the American camp. Major Francis Ross led Fergus and sixty other horsemen to Paris's Mill on March 1. Fergus said that a local woman informed them that British troops encamped nearby would soon drive the Americans out of the area.

The horsemen returned to camp on March 2. Ashe returned from Purrysburg a few hours after Ross returned from Paris's Mill, but did not consult with Ross until later in the day. Either Ross did not tell Ashe that British troops were on the way or Ashe did not believe the intelligence to be accurate. Ross apparently told Ashe that his men were exhausted from their long march and overnight scouting expedition, so Ashe did not order them to scout on the night of March 2. The Americans, therefore, did not discover that a British force was bearing down on them from Paris's Mill.[4]

On the morning of March 3, Ashe sent Ross with about 160 horsemen to scout the area between Brier Creek and Hudson's Ferry. While Ross was on patrol, he found evidence that British troops were on the move towards Paris's Mill, but he did not relay the information to the American camp at Brier Creek.

Fergus remained at Brier Creek with about forty of the horsemen who had ridden to Paris's Mill two days earlier. Fergus and his comrades camped in an old field where they could take care of their horses; the field was about a quarter-mile from the main American encampment.[5]

Colonel Leonard Marbury, a veteran of the campaigns along the Georgia-Florida frontier, led a band of dragoons on a reconnaissance mission toward Paris's Mill. The dragoons encountered British troops and exchanged shots. Marbury attempted to send a messenger to warn the Americans at the camp on Brier Creek, but the British captured the messenger. Another American horsemen, however, also saw the British force and raced back to the camp. Shortly after he arrived, a messenger came from the detachment guarding the baggage train at Burton's Ferry eight miles from the encampment and reported that a large British force was approaching the American position.[6]

ELBERT AND Bryant joined Ashe for a quick conference. They agreed that the Americans would have to stand and fight.

The Americans distributed ammunition under imminent threat of attack. Some of the soldiers received ammunition that did not match the caliber of their weapons. Because the soldiers did not have cartridge boxes, they stuffed ammunition into their shirts or cradled cartridges in their elbows.

The British force reached the American camp at 3 p.m. on March 3, 1779, and drove back the pickets. As the Americans scrambled to take defensive positions, the British infantry advanced at the quick step and the British artillery opened fire.[7] Ashe told Elbert "Sir, you had better advance and engage them."[8]

About nine hundred British soldiers attacked the American camp. Captain Baird's light infantry faced the American left flank along the Brier Creek swamp. The 2nd Battalion of the 71st occupied the center. North Carolina provincials and Florida Rangers faced the American right flank. Fifty loyalist riflemen took position to shoot down patriots attempting to flee toward the Savannah River. The grenadiers of the 60th Regiment and dragoons led by Thomas Trawse stood by in reserve. Colonel James Mark Prevost placed his five artillery pieces in the center, to the rear of the 2nd Battalion of the 71st Highlanders.[9]

American rosters listed about eleven hundred troops at Brier Creek, but detachments had reduced the number significantly; there may have been as few as six hundred troops in the main encampment. Elbert occupied the center of the American line with his Georgia Continentals and militia, totaling about a hundred. North Carolina militia from New Bern formed on the left beside Brier Creek, while North Carolina militia from Edenton took position on the right toward the Savannah River swamp. North Carolina militia from Halifax and Wilmington formed the second line.

The entire battle lasted only about fifteen minutes, and most of the Americans fled within five minutes after the initial attack. Elbert's Georgians fired two volleys, and the British returned fire. Then, according to Ashe, the Georgians "advanced without orders a few steps beyond the line and moved to the left in front of the regiment from the district of New Bern, which much impeded their firing." The militia from Edenton moved slightly to the right. The combined movements of the Georgians to the left and the North Carolinians to the right created a gap in the American line.[10]

The troops in the center of the British line launched a bayonet charge into the gap. Many of the American militiamen ran away without firing a shot. The Wilmington men and some of the New Bern men fired a few volleys and stood their ground waiting for reinforcements. The militia unit from Edenton fled from the British bayonets, and the rest of the North Carolina militia panicked and joined the flight. Elbert realized that the American right wing had evaporated when he discovered British soldiers attacking his soldiers from behind his position.[11]

Fergus and his forty fellow horsemen were summoned to the battlefield. "The line was just formed as we arrived to the left wing commanded by Colonel Elbert," Fergus said. "We rode close along the rear of the line when the first general fire was made; as we were on lower ground than the enemy, it passed chiefly over our heads. We had got to the extremity of the right wing where General Ashe commanded by the time the second fire was made. This was our post, but we had not time to give more than one fire when the general wheeled and fled and the whole wing with him. He was gone about 150 yards or more before our little party followed."[12]

Lytle's detachment rushed from its position at Miller Bridge and came within a hundred yards of the British line; two of Lytle's men were wounded. Lytle's men moved against a tide of Americans fleeing into the swamps. Lytle tried to march his men from the battlefield in good military order.[13]

The battle gave the Highlanders in the British force an occasion to avenge the death of Hugh MacAlister, the sergeant whose body had been hacked with hatchets in Augusta. Archibald Campbell, who received second-hand accounts of the battle, wrote in his journal: "…when the light infantry were running up in line to charge the rebels, one of the Highlanders called out – *Now my Boys, remember poor Macalister:* in consequence of which, this corps spared very few that came within their reach."[14]

While the other Americans fled, Elbert motivated his band of Continental troops and Georgia militia to keep fighting until they were killed, wounded, or captured. Elbert suffered a gunshot wound before he surrendered.[15]

FERGUS AND other Americans fleeing from battle sloshed through three miles of swamp to reach the Savannah River. "General Ashe rode a good horse, left his men, and got round the enemy and made to a ferry above, crossed, and escaped," Fergus said, "while the rest of us were drove into the swamp between the creek and the river. The banks of these were so steep and deep that the horses that went in could not get out again, and some men would have been drowned had not canes been put into their hands and helped them out. We now got into a thick canebreak, and the enemy pursued us no farther. This was late in the evening. Twelve of us got together, and, as it was moonlight in the night, we formed a small raft of driftwood in the mouth of a lagoon, on which three of us with danger and much difficulty got over the river, after being carried above a mile down before we landed."

On the South Carolina side of the river, Fergus said, "We got out of the bottom and wandered up the river till daylight." Fergus and his comrades found a rowboat loaded with ears of corn. "Opposite to us on the other bank we discovered a great number of the North Carolina men," Fergus said. Risking their safety for the sake of soldiers stranded on the Georgia side, Fergus and his comrades "quickly rowed over and took in as many as the boat would bear and caused them to throw out the corn while we crossed back. By this means we got all our men that were there off before the enemy came down to the river." [16]

"Poor fellows!" exclaimed General William Moultrie, who was stationed downriver at Purrysburg at the time of the battle. "Most of them threw down their arms," Moultrie said, "and ran through a deep swamp, two or three miles, to gain the banks of a wide and rapid river, and plunged themselves in, to escape from the bayonet; many of them endeavoring to reach the opposite shore, sunk down, and were buried in a watery grave; while those who had more strength, and skill in swimming, gained the other side, but were still so terrified, that they straggled through the woods in every direction."[17]

The Americans who crossed the river continued to suffer. Fergus observed, "Many of our men were half-naked, having stripped to swim the river. The third of March we were defeated, and that night there was a light frost, and many suffered in the cold, having nothing on but a shirt or breeches. Here we lay, I know not how long."[18]

As the survivors of the Battle of Brier Creek emerged from the swamps on the South Carolina side of the Savannah River, they not only showed that they had lost confidence in Ashe's leadership but also behaved more like refugees than soldiers. American officers tried to restore military order.

Moultrie reported that Captain Peter Horry came upon several hundred fugitives, most of them without their weapons, rushing along in confusion. Ashe asked Horry to stop the men because they were running away. Bryant said they were not running away. Ashe insisted they were. Horry asked whether Ashe or Bryant was the commanding officer and learned that Ashe held the higher rank. "Then, sir, I will obey your orders," Horry told Ashe. Horry ordered his men to present fixed bayonets and threatened to fire upon the fugitives if they attempted to come forward. Then Horry continued to American headquarters at Purrysburg with his detachment. Ashe and Bryant followed with the fugitives.[19]

Because Ashe fled the battlefield during his ignominious defeat at Brier Creek, some of his fellow Americans cast aspersions on his ability as a commander and his courage as a soldier. With his honor at stake, Ashe asked for an opportunity to explain his side of the story. He was granted a court martial. "He acknowledged that he galloped off the field whilst the Georgians were still engaged," Moultrie reported, "but adds that it was in order to get in front of his own people, with a view of rallying them, and that finding, after riding after them near three quarters of a mile, that they could not be stopped, and that either death or captivity must be his fate, if he persisted, he had entered the swamp in order to make his escape towards the ferry."[20]

The court martial gave Ashe a half-hearted vindication. While concluding that Ashe "did not take all the necessary precautions which he ought to have done to secure his camp, and obtain timely intelligence of the movements and approach of the enemy," the court acquitted him "of every imputation of a want of personal courage in the affair at Brier Creek, and think he remained in the field as long as prudence and duty required."[21]

THE BRITISH SCORED a decisive victory at the Battle of Brier Creek. Their casualties were relatively light: one British officer and five privates died in the battle, and ten British soldiers suffered wounds.

The British captured the American artillery – accounts range from two swivel guns to seven field pieces – about a thousand muskets and all of the American supplies, provisions and equipment. One soldier fled so quickly that he left his boots in camp. The fleeing Americans discarded hundreds of hats, shirts, canteens and firearms on the banks of the river. Forced to choose between clothes and a rifle, many soldiers chose to keep their rifles as they prepared to plunge into the cold, swift, deep water.[22]

American casualties at the Battle of Brier Creek have been estimated at nearly two hundred either killed in battle or drowned. Exact figures are not available, partly because most of the survivors walked to their homes in North Carolina without stopping anywhere along the way.[23]

Throughout the war, commanders often exaggerated their successes, and that may have been the case when Augustine Prevost boasted that "Brigadier General Elbert, one of their best officers, several more of note, in the whole twenty-seven officers, were taken, with near two hundred men." Prevost reported "about 150 killed on the field of battle and adjoining woods and swamps; but their chief loss consists in the number of officers and men drowned in attempting to save themselves from the slaughter, and plunging into a deep and rapid river."[24]

Chapter 4

Afterword

THE BRITISH VICTORY AT BRIER CREEK carried significant consequences. British officials continued to implement colonial rule in Georgia, and exiled Governor James Wright returned to Savannah on July 14, 1779, four months after the battle. The British military maintained control of Savannah and coastal Georgia until the war was practically finished. From their base in Savannah, the British moved northward, captured Charleston, and set up a chain of posts across the South Carolina backcountry. The British occupied Augusta from May of 1780 until June of 1781, temporarily exerting control over all of Georgia. Those gains would have been stopped or at least delayed if the American campaign to wrest Georgia from British control had not ended in disaster at Brier Creek.

American General William Moultrie recognized the significance of the Battle of Brier Creek in the progress of the American Revolution. "This unlucky affair at Brier Creek disconcerted all our plans," Moultrie said, "and through the misfortunes of General Howe and General Ashe the war was protracted at least one year longer."[1]

ARCHIBALD CAMPBELL WAITED at Savannah for a ship to take him to England. He wanted to go home to marry his fiancée and to manage his personal affairs, which had fallen into disarray while he was a prisoner of war in America for two years before he was exchanged and assigned to conquer Georgia.[2]

On March 6, three days after the Battle of Brier Creek, Campbell learned that the British had defeated the Americans.

"The defeat at Briar Creek was productive of good consequences," Campbell said, "as the whole of the rebels after this discomfiture withdrew themselves to South Carolina and united their chief force under General Lincoln at Purrysburg, excepting a small detachment stationed at Augusta."[3]

Campbell embarked on a warship that sailed from Savannah on March 13 and reached Plymouth, England, on May 14. Two days later he met with Lord George Germain, the Secretary of State for the Colonies. Germain had written a letter to Campbell in March, but Campbell did not receive a copy of the letter until he reached England in May. British officials were encouraged, Germain wrote, "by knowing you were to command the troops appointed for the expedition to Georgia, to expect that every advantage would be derived from it which the exertion of great abilities, improved by a thorough knowledge of the military science, at the head of troops distinguished by their intrepid valour, would obtain."

Germain praised "the arrangements you had made for the security of the province and the establishment of good order and tranquility among the loyal inhabitants," calling them "equally judicious with the measure you had taken for its conquest."

On May 17 Campbell met with King George III, "kissed hands, and was most graciously received." Germain told Campbell that "His Majesty was most graciously pleased to declare that the rapidity of your success had exceeded his hopes" and that Campbell's achievements earned the king's "fullest approbation."[4]

Soon after arriving in London, Campbell received a letter from Sir Henry Clinton, the British commander in America. "Your establishment of civil government," Clinton said, was "highly proper." Clinton told Campbell "Your success has been completed."[5]

Writing from America, General Augustine Prevost gave Campbell credit for conceiving the strategy to impose military control over Georgia, although he gave his brother James Mark Prevost the credit for planning and executing the attack at Brier Creek. "I have before now expressed to your lordship how much I felt to be deprived of the assistance of an officer of Colonel Campbell's merit," Augustine Prevost told Germain. "Indeed it was not till after repeated solicitations and his mentioning his being unwell that I could possibly see him give up the execution of a plan formed by himself." The American army's advance to Brier Creek, as Campbell predicted, "drew them into that snare," Augustine Prevost wrote, "which was so fatal to them, so glorious to His Majesty's troops, and honourable to Lieut-Colonel Prevost who planned and executed it so judiciously."[6]

The issue of rank continued to irritate Campbell. Germain told him "It gave me much concern to find that the jealousies of the senior officers should have interposed to prevent Sir Henry Clinton from giving you the extraordinary rank he had intended, and to which your merit so well entitles you." Germain continued, "I trust it will not be long before he will find an opportunity of gratifying your wishes and his own inclination."[7]

Campbell's wishes were gratified on December 8, 1779, ten months after the Battle of Brier Creek, when he was promoted to the rank of brigadier general in Jamaica. He was appointed lieutenant governor of Jamaica in 1781 and appointed governor in 1782. He retired from service in Jamaica in 1784, and the next year was created a Knight of the Bath. He served as governor of Madras in India from 1786 to 1789 and also commanded the 74th Highlanders in 1787. In 1790 he was appointed Hereditary Usher of the White Rod. He died in 1791 and was buried in Westminster Abbey.[8]

JAMES FERGUS KNEW how to live to fight another day, but he had some close calls. Born in 1756, he participated in the early battles of the American Revolution in 1776 and survived the disaster at Brier Creek in 1779.[9]

Immediately after the Battle of Brier Creek, Fergus took twelve wagons to Saluda to obtain flour for the American army on the Savannah River. About a month after the battle, he was discharged and returned home to Camden.[10]

When British General Augustine Prevost invaded South Carolina a year after the Battle of Brier Creek, Fergus volunteered once again and reported for duty at Orangeburg. After marching for ten days and crossing the Edisto River twice, he reached Charleston. Fergus "hoped to have a night's rest after our fatiguing march, but an alarm took place and we had to lie on the lines all night."

Two weeks later, Fergus participated in maneuvers and skirmishes around Dorchester near Charleston. For three days he "had not sleep or rest," he said, "drinking bad water and enduring the scorching sun by day and the chilling dews by night." After enduring these conditions, Fergus contracted a high fever.

Fergus knew that if he were to live to fight another day, he would have to stay out of military hospitals. "I sent into Charleston to Dr. David Ramsay, who I understood was principal of the hospital in the city, for some medicine," Fergus said. "He sent it, but advised me to be brought into the hospital. I replied that I had seen the hospitals in Philadelphia, Princeton, and Newark and would prefer dying in the open air of the woods rather than be stifled to death in a crowded hospital."

A relative invited Fergus to recuperate at a house in Charleston. "I was taken there in a wagon," Fergus later recalled, "and by the time I got in I was partly insensible. My friend brought the doctor to see me, and he ordered what he thought proper and called duly morning and evening to see me until the fever was broke. How long that was, I know not now. It appears like a dream to me now." Years after the war when he was filing a pension application, Fergus wrote "To the great care and attention of the humane and kindhearted Dr. Ramsay, under God, I am indebted for my being a living, though infirm, old man at this day."[11]

Fergus recuperated at Charleston for about ten months before returning to his parents in the upper part of South Carolina. He had lived to fight another day. After the British captured Charleston in 1780 and established posts across South Carolina, Fergus served under Thomas Sumter and other partisan leaders "dispersing and keeping down the Tories," he said. "It was a perilous time, and we were in a continual state of warfare until after Cornwallis surrendered, in which warfare I had my share."[12]

After his fighting days were over, Fergus lived to the age of 81.[13]

AFTER SAMUEL ELBERT surrendered at Brier Creek, he was paroled at Sunbury during the summer and fall of 1779. The officers on parole could rent residences, find employment, and sometimes travel to Savannah.

When British forces abandoned Sunbury in September to reinforce Savannah, the American officers became vulnerable to marauding loyalists, who succeeded in killing one Continental captain. The American officers also suffered from scarcities of food and supplies.

In the aftermath of the disastrous Siege of Savannah, American forces withdrew into South Carolina and Continental General Benjamin Lincoln advised the officers at Sunbury to move to safety while still being considered prisoners of war on parole. By October, all of the officers had left Sunbury.[14]

More than two years after he was taken prisoner, Elbert was exchanged in June of 1781.

Elbert accepted a position as commander of arms and stores in George Washington's army and participated in the decisive victory at Yorktown. Elbert faced a familiar opponent, the 2nd Regiment of the 71st Regiment, and found a familiar ally, James Fergus. As Elbert and Fergus discussed their experiences at Brier

Creek, Fergus learned that Elbert "fully believed General Ashe betrayed us to the British, and declared that if he ever met with him, one of them should die before they parted."[15]

PART TWO

LEGENDS

A legend is a piece of mythology or folklore that refers to historical persons and events. From a strictly historical perspective, the following stories taken from previously published sources may be true, mostly true, partly true or original creations from the imaginations of the storytellers.

Chapter 5

An Accusation of Atrocities

AN ANONYMOUS ACCOUNT accuses the 71st Highlanders of committing atrocities that today would be called war crimes. The person who wrote the account got information from another person who visited the Brier Creek Battlefield after the battle was over. Historians who have used the manuscript as a source have given two slightly different citations: Draper microfilm, volume 13DD33, on file at Kings Mountain National Military Park; Draper Microfilm Collection, 3 DD 89-91, State Historical Society of Wisconsin, Madison.

A copy of the hand-written account provided by Alex Lee of Sylvania has notes in the margin asking if the accusations are true and hinting that they may be anti-Scottish propaganda.

THROUGHOUT HISTORY, Scottish Highlanders have been considered fierce warriors. The Highlanders of the 71st Regiment maintained that reputation at Long Island, New York, in August of 1776. "The Hessians and our brave Highlanders gave no quarters," one of their officers observed, "and it was a fine sight to see with what alacrity they dispatched the rebels with their bayonets, after we had surrounded them so they could not resist." Another British officer, however, was "greatly shocked at the massacre made by the Hessians and Highlanders after victory was decided."[1]

On several occasions, atrocities were attributed to Sir James Baird, an aristocratic Lowlander Scot who led the light troops at Brier Creek. When the accuser in the Brier Creek case says "Sir James Baird of the 71st... is known in the northern part of America, as well as in these for his unfeeling heart and relentless cruelty" he may have been referring, notes William E. Cox, "to an incident that supposedly happened in a little village in Jamaica, New York." Cox explains:

> The story is that General Woodhull and two companions were captured in an inn by a party of British under Sir James Baird. Tradition says that Baird ordered Woodhull to shout "God save the King!" and because he shouted "God save us all," Baird struck him with his broadsword and would have killed him if Major Delancey, who accompanied Baird, had not interfered. Woodhull later died from the blows delivered by Baird.[2]

Another historian believes the tale is untrue or only partly true:

> There is a tradition that when Sir James Baird's men captured General Nathaniel Woodhull on Long Island, the Scotch officer ordered him to shout, "God save the King!" The American having cried instead, "God save us all!" Baird struck him with his broadsword, mangling Woodhull's arm. (B.J. Lossing. *The Pictorial Fieldbook of the Revolution.* 2 vols., New York, 1860: II, 811 n.) The tale is at best doubtful. It seems more likely that the New York patriot was wounded in attempting to escape. During a night attack in New Jersey Baird's troops butchered a number of Americans trapped in a farm house, an affair described as "one of the most disgraceful" of the Revolution (*New York Archives – Newspaper Extracts,* 1778: III, 457 n.)[3]

"It has been said that [Baird] was the officer who attacked and mortally wounded Brigadier General Nathaniel Woodhull after the latter's capture on Long Island, August 28, 1776," writes Colin Campbell. "All commentators on the matter seem to have ignored the fact that Baird was still in England, and about to set out for America, on June 14, 1776."[4]

Baird's dubious reputation in the North followed him to the South. His men were accused of rioting and pillaging after the capture of Savannah. Mordecai Sheftall described Baird's treatment of civilians:

> I endeavored, with my son Sheftall, to make our escape across Musgrove Creek... But on our arrival at the creek, after having sustained a very heavy fire of musketry from the light infantry under the command of Sir James Baird during the time we were crossing the common, without any injury to either of us, we found it high water. And my son not knowing how to swim, and we with about 186 officers and privates being caught as it were in a pen, and the Highlanders keeping up a constant fire on us, it was thought advisable to surrender ourselves prisoners, which we accordingly did and which was no sooner done than the Highlanders plundered every one amongst us except Major Low, myself and my son, who, being foremost, had an opportunity to surrender ourselves to the British officer, namely Lieutenant Peter Campbell, who disarmed us as we came into the yard formerly occupied by Mr. Moses Nunes.
>
> During this business Sir James Baird was missing but, on his coming into the yard, he mounted himself on the stepladder which was erected at the end of the house and sounded his brass bugle horn, which the

Highlanders no sooner heard than they all got about him, when he addressed himself to them in Highland language, when they all dispersed and finished plundering such of the officers and men who had been fortunate enough to escape their first search.[5]

A teenage girl who lived in Savannah at the time of the battle reported:

...the Americans as they retreated wantonly fired on the 71st Regiment of Highlanders, without attempting a regular stand. This exposed the inhabitants to the fury of the British soldiers, who then felt as though they were taking the place by storm. In consequence, before the officers could have time to stop them they committed much outrage, ripped open feather beds, destroyed the public papers and records, and scattered everything about the streets. Numbers of the enemy were taken in a swamp a few miles from Savannah. While Mr. Johnston was with his [loyalist] company in the pursuit he saw his father at his own door, and had only time to go up to Colonel Maitland [of the 71st Regiment] and request that he would put a guard at his father's house to secure his safety from the enraged troops, who knew not friend from foe. Colonel Maitland had been the early friend and college companion of my father-in-law Dr. Johnston, in Edinburgh, and meeting with his son at New York was like a father to him and did all he could to serve him. He, of course, placed a guard there.

My father in a few days sent a passport for myself and my aunt to come to town. I was then in my fifteenth year, and new to scenes of the kind, and having to stop within a mile of Savannah that the Hessian officer on duty there should examine our pass, I was dreadfully frightened. He soon allowed us to go on; and what a sight did the streets present of feathers and papers!

The meeting with my father I scarce need add was joyful...[6]

Although the British commander reported "few or no depredations occurred," other witnesses claimed that British soldiers stabbed defenseless Americans repeatedly with bayonets, stole property, destroyed public records, and smashed fine furniture.[7]

In a report delivered to Congress, the governor of Georgia claimed: "the spirit of Rapine Insolence and Brutality indulged in by the soldiery, exceeds Description... People who have got out of Town since the Action say [the British commanders] profess great humanity, and totally disavow many horrid Acts committed by their People... for my Part I wish to leave nothing to their Humanity and as little to their Justice."[8]

There were horror stories about British treatment of civilians in Savannah: "Robbery, incendiarism, rape and murder were the fruits of that unhappy day," wrote a witness to the British capture of Savannah.[9]

At Brier Creek, Archibald Campbell's assertion that Baird's light infantrymen "spared very few that came within their reach" is balanced by Augustine Prevost's report that the British took two hundred prisoners.[10]

After the British Parliament heard accounts of Sir James Baird's conduct, he was recalled from the American field of action. He returned to Europe in the summer of 1779, a few months after the Battle of Brier Creek, and from that point the 71st Regiment restored its reputation.[11]

EVEN IF THE ACCOUNT of atrocities at Brier Creek is not historically accurate, the account contributes to the legend of the battle. Portions of the hand-written account are illegible, and an author who transcribed it placed clarifying material in brackets:

> ...Many parties of the Americans finding the day lost, threw down their arms and begged for quarter; but alas! they found none.
> The merciless 71st and light infantry boasted of sheathing their bayonets in the bosoms of these poor supplicants.
> The gentleman who gave this detail saw the next morning on the field and adjoining many clusters of Americans who had been massacred on their knees praying for quarter, most of their bodies disfigured with reiterated gashes and stabs.
> Sir James Baird of the 71st, whose name is known in the northern parts of America, as well as in these for his unfeeling heart and relentless cruelty, vaunted [or recounted] of having put to death nearly a dozen of these supplicants with his own hands, and eventually [?] showed their blood oozing out of the touchhole of his fusee.
> But what particularly added to the horrors of the field was that portion of the 71st in the night, after plundering the camp set afire (through sport) to the booth [brush?] hut where the American sick were, and where a number of the wounded had crawled to by way of sanctuary from the highlanders as well as to screen themselves from the inclemency of the night. Their half consumed, their parched and blackening bodies joined the next morning in offering a sight such perhaps as the sun seldom rises upon among the civi-

lized nations. His nature (said the gentleman) sickened at the sight of so many spectacles of cruelty, and he turned with disgust from the scene.

His humanity soon after must have received an additional shock which language indeed can but weakly describe. It was about 14 or 15 wounded Americans that had been brought together under a pine tree, by some of the humane English in order, as he supposed to have their wounds dressed; but alas! they never experienced the Doctor's Aid. Twas 1 o'clock when the shade having moved from off them, they were exposed to a very burning sun, at the same time come up a 71st officer, and his party passing, stopped likewise to view them; several were just expiring and others appeared to be in the agonies of death. The rest that were able to speak joined in supplicating their pity and begged the soldiers for a little water from their canteens. Can it be believed that their piteous situation, their gaping wounds, their convulsed frames and agonizing tears, moved not these men's pity. Their prayers were answered with damns and wishes that all rebels were in the same predicament; and the party marched off without giving a drop of water to cool their parched lips.[12]

Chapter 6

Legendary Last-second Rescues

A LEGEND ARISING from the Battle of Brier Creek tells how Samuel Elbert and John McIntosh escaped death through the last-minute intervention of British officers.

A Georgia history book published in 1900 gives this version of the legend:

> The only ray of light that shone through the darkness of this sad defeat was shed by the bravery of Col. Elbert and his command. He fought until he was struck down, and he was on the point of being killed by a soldier with uplifted bayonet when he made the masonic sign of distress. An officer noticed it, responded instantly, stayed the soldier's arm, and saved Col. Elbert's life.
>
> As a prisoner on parole, in the British camp, he was treated with great respect and kindness. Honor and reward were promised him if he would join the British, but all such offers were promptly rejected.
>
> Col. McIntosh, the hero of Fort Morris, had stood his ground with Col. Elbert until nearly every man was killed, and then he was captured. As he was surrendering his sword, a British officer tried to kill him; and he was saved by the timely interference of his kinsman, Sir Aeneas McIntosh, of the British army.[1]

Another Georgia historian says that Elbert's felicitous facility in signaling saved his life not once but twice:

The brave Colonel was himself struck down and was about to be dispatched by a bayonet thrust, when he gave the Masonic sign of distress. An officer saw it and instantly responded and Colonel Elbert's life was saved by the benevolent principal of brotherly love.

While a prisoner... inducements were tendered him with the hope of winning him to the British cause; and when all these failed, an attempt was made by two Indians to take his life. He fortunately discovered them in time and gave them a signal which he had formerly been accustomed to use among them. Their guns were immediately lowered and they came forward to shake his hand. This signal had probably been agreed upon and used when... he guarded the Indian Chiefs back to the Creek Nation. In former years, in his mercantile relations with the Indians, he had been a great favorite among them.[2]

Several Georgia historians tell the legend of Colonel Samuel Elbert being rescued when he made the Masonic sign of distress. A marker placed at Brier Creek by the Grand Lodge of Georgia Free and Accepted Masons repeats the story and adds that Elbert was the Grand Master of the lodge at the time of the battle.[3]

"The credibility of the story suffers on several counts," writes historian David S. Heidler, who points out that the story is not included in either British or American accounts of the battle. Heidler writes:

...the event itself seems unrealistic. The British were not in the habit of killing high-ranking Continental officers who were attempting to surrender, both for reasons of tradition and for the practical reason that such captives were valuable commodities in prisoner exchanges. The British knew Elbert and respected his abilities... Therefore, the Masonic distress story most probably is nothing more than legend.[4]

Viewed from another perspective, the Masonic distress story is nothing less than legend.

Confluence of Cannon Lake and Brier Creek

Chapter 7

The Legend of Cannon Lake

A LOCAL LEGEND tells how an oxbow lake on Brier Creek got the name Cannon Lake. On a visit to Cannon Lake in 1999, Lamar Zipperer provided a handout with a summary of the legend:

> The story of Cannon Lake in brief is that during February 28-March 3 of 1779, the British forces were traveling hurriedly from Hudson's Ferry toward Augusta. While crossing the creek on a bridge (Freeman's Bridge on the old Augusta Road), they lost a cannon in the creek waters. Thus, the small oxbow lake near the bridge

is called Cannon Lake. Some people say that a cannon was too valuable to be left behind and the British probably recovered it from the water. Others say that the cannon is still in the water, and old timers spin yarns about swimming, diving and playing around it as children.

If indeed the cannon is still there, it probably is in the creek, <u>not</u> the lake, because the bridge crossed the creek not the lake.[1]

Like any legend, this tale may be partly truth and partly fiction, because the historical record says the British did, indeed, lose an artillery piece in the creek.

William Moultrie of Charleston, a general who was stationed with the Southern department of the Continental army downstream of Brier Creek on the Savannah River at Purrysburg at the time of the battle, mentioned the incident in a letter he wrote to Colonel Charles Pinckney on February 27, 1779:

> ... the enemy retreated so precipitately from Augusta, as to leave twelve beef killed and skinned upon the ground; ...a panic seized them, and they pushed for Brier-creek, which they accomplished before our horse-men could destroy the bridge, and they passed it, they burnt it down to prevent our pursuit, they lost one field-piece in crossing, by the boat sinking: Gen. Ash has sent to have it taken up and brought to his camp... [2]

An article published in *The Georgia Historical Quarterly* in 1926 says Moultrie's letter "gave rise to the tradition, yet current, that a cannon was thrown into the creek where the bridge had been, and that it has never been recovered, though several searches have been made for it."[3]

Chapter 8

The Adventures of John McIntosh

LIEUTENANT COLONEL JOHN MCINTOSH looked out from the parapet and saw an old man strutting outside the walls of Fort Morris at Sunbury, Georgia. The old man wore a British uniform and brandished a claymore, a huge sword favored by warriors from the Scottish Highlands. McIntosh recognized the man. They were relatives and, before the American Revolution, they had lived on neighboring plantations. The old man was Roderick McIntosh, called Rory, and he was obviously drunk.

"Surrender, you miscreants!" Rory demanded. "How dare you presume to resist his Majesty's arms?"

John told his men not to shoot. Trying to get Rory out of harm's way, John opened the gate to the fort and said, "Walk in, Mr. McIntosh, and take possession."

"No," Rory said. "I will not trust myself among such vermin, but I order you to surrender."

Someone shot at Rory, and the ball passed through his face under his eyes. He stumbled and fell, but quickly stood up. He put his hand to one cheek, looked at the blood on his hand, and then raised his hand to the other cheek and discovered that it also was covered in blood. He backed away from the fort, flourishing his sword. Several more shots rang out. Someone shouted, "Run, they'll kill you!"

Rory replied, "I come from a people who never run."

Continuing to face the enemy and still flourishing his sword, Rory stepped backward into the safety of the British lines.[1]

Like most legends, that one may be partly true. John and Rory McIntosh were kinsmen and former neighbors; John was the highest-ranking Continental officer at Fort Morris during the siege of 1778; Rory was a captain in the British army at St. Augustine; and Rory was present at Fort Morris on occasion during the war.

The historical record indicates that Rory McIntosh's exploits at Sunbury took place during the second siege of Sunbury in January of 1779 rather than during the first siege two months previously. A British officer who was at Sunbury in January of 1779 mentioned Rory in a memoir:

> ...Mr. Roderic Mackintosh accompanied by his faithful Negro Cyrus, disdaining the counsel of Cyrus, walked under the musketry of the Garrison, setting them at defiance, when they shot him down and disarmed him so quickly that Lieutenant Baron Breitenbach and Sergeant Supman of the 4th. Battalion Light Infantry who with alacrity ran to his rescue could only carry him in wounded in the face. As soon as our men seized him the Americans ceased firing...
>
> ...a shell fell upon a building where the rebel officers messed, and killed and wounded 9 of them, and shattered about 50 stand of arms; upon which they proposed to capitulate; which being refused and 2 more shells falling into the fort, they hauled down their colours and surrendered at discretion... The Garrison with their Commander Major Lane embarked for Savannah... Lieutenant Colonel Allen was left at Sunbury with the Jersey Volunteers. Mr. Mackintosh was appointed Captain of the Fort, he lost the use of his eye.[2]

JOHN MCINTOSH WAS A GRANDSON of John Mackintosh Mor, the leader of the Highlanders who founded Darien, Georgia. When the American Revolution erupted, John McIntosh and his father William McIntosh joined the American cause. John McIntosh became a captain in the 1st Georgia Regiment on January 7, 1776, under the command of his uncle Lachlan McIntosh. John was promoted to major in September of 1776. He was just 23 years old on April 1, 1778, when he was promoted to lieutenant colonel commanding the 3rd Battalion of the Georgia Continental Line. He served on the Florida-Georgia frontier and participated in a Council of War on July 11, 1778, at Fort Tonyn during the third expedition to Florida [3]

In November of 1778, John McIntosh was the ranking Continental officer at Fort Morris in Sunbury, Georgia, when British and loyalist forces besieged the fort.

When the British commander issued a summons to surrender the fort, McIntosh replied:

> We acknowledge we are not ignorant that your army is in motion to endeavor to reduce this State. We believe it entirely chimerical that Colonel Prevost is at the Meeting-House: but should it be so, we are in no degree apprehensive of danger from a junction of his army with yours. We have no property compared with the object we contend for that we value a rush; and would rather perish in a vigorous defense than accept your proposals. We, Sir, are fighting the battles of America, and therefore disdain to remain neutral till its fate is determined. As to surrendering the fort, receive this laconic reply: Come and take it.[4]

The British commander called off the siege and sailed back to Florida.

The Georgia legislature was so impressed with the conspicuous gallantry of Colonel McIntosh that it presented him a sword engraved with the words "Come and Take It."[5]

THREE MONTHS AFTER DEFENDING Sunbury, McIntosh enlarged his legendary status by making a determined stand at the Battle of Brier Creek. He was taken prisoner after nearly all the men under his command had been killed or captured.

McIntosh remained a prisoner of war for more than a year; he apparently was paroled, because in May of 1780 he was in Augusta. He was exchanged sometime after June of 1780 for Lieutenant Colonel John Harris Cruger.[6]

Although McIntosh was a Continental officer, he volunteered to serve with the Georgia militia through the campaign of 1781 and for a time was an aide to the South Carolina partisan leader General Thomas Sumter.[7]

LEGENDARY DEEDS WERE ASCRIBED to the dashing young officer. For instance, the story goes, in 1781 he fought a duel with Lieutenant Augustus George Christian Elholm.[8] Here is a romantic account of that deed:

> ...McIntosh, when a Lieutenant Colonel in the army of the Revolution, during the war became acquainted with Miss Sarah Swinton, of South Carolina, of Scottish descent, and whose father, a patriot of those times, was killed in battle by the British at Stono. Her form was light and delicate. Possessed of a well-cultivated and discriminating mind, with a rare faculty for conversation and argument, and although of retiring manners, she espoused with an almost imprudent zeal the cause of freedom, in a part of the country infested by Tories, and marauding bands of British troops. To this lady he was engaged to be married; and in one of his excursions to the neighbourhood in which she resided, he was informed that Captain Elholm, a Polander in the American service (Lee's Legion), had acted oppressively towards some of the inhabitants, and on remonstrating with him on the in-

justice and impolicy of his conduct, a quarrel quickly ensued, and which, it was promptly determined, should be settled by the arbitrament of the sword.

... Both were young, resolute, active, and powerful men, and it was thought that one or both would certainly be killed in the contest; and as the parties were moving to the place of combat, Miss Swinton requested to see for an instant her intended consort... He called on her, and was met with serious distress, and after a little conversation, she observed, "If you are, then, inviolably pledged to meet this man, and feel that your honour is dearer than life, what shall I do?" [She soon] fled to her room, to conceal there her agitation and the anguish of a devoted heart.

The hostile parties met under a large oak... At the word "Ready," they drew, and, advancing with sharp and glittering swords, commenced the battle in good earnest, with firm hearts and sturdy arms. In a little time the right arm of Captain Elholm was nearly severed from his body, and fell powerless by his side. ...His sword was dexterously transferred to his left hand, which he used with great effect; and the blows came so awkwardly, that they were not easily parried by his right-handed antagonist. Both were in a few moments disabled in such a manner, that the friends present felt it proper to interfere, and end the bloody conflict.

They carried to their graves the scars, and deeply furrowed cheeks, as evidences of a once terrible struggle. Miss Swinton was not long in suspense; the combatants were soon taken from the field, disfigured by many deep and dangerous sabre wounds, of which, in due time, they both recovered; and the Colonel often remarked that he was more indebted to the tender attentions of Miss S. for his restoration to health than to the management or skill of his surgeon...

A little time after this occurrence, Colonel McIntosh brought his young and patriotic wife to Georgia, his native State... [9]

JOHN AND SARAH MARRIED on June 17, 1781, in Colleton County, South Carolina.[10] John brought Sarah to Georgia and they had six children. He received a commission as a major in the Glynn County Militia in 1790.

Later, John and Sarah McIntosh moved to the St. Johns River in Florida. During their residence in Florida, Sarah lost her eyesight in an accident. John was arrested on suspicion of activities against the Spanish government, and was imprisoned first at St. Augustine and then in Havana for a year. While John was imprisoned, "the private influence of General Washington, and of the most distinguished men of our country, many of whom had served with [John] during the war, was exerted in his behalf, mainly through the active correspondence and ceaseless efforts of Mrs. McIntosh."[11]

After Spanish officials released McIntosh from captivity, he and his devoted wife Sarah returned to Georgia.

Sarah's health continued to decline and she died in 1799 on St. Simons Island.

McIntosh later married Agnes Hightower Hillary, widow of Revolutionary War officer and Georgia statesman Christopher Hillary; John's son William married the widow's daughter, Maria.[12]

MCINTOSH WAS COMMISSIONED as a major general in the Georgia Militia in 1809.[13] During the War of 1812 he commanded a division of the Georgia Militia in federal service from December of 1814 through May of 1815. The division included: the 1st Brigade of Georgia Militia; the 2nd Brigade, which was stationed at

Fort Barrington on the Altamaha River; the 4th Regiment, stationed at Fort Decatur; and a battalion of artillery assigned to protect coastal Georgia.[14]

When the British threatened the Gulf Coast, McIntosh engaged in active service at Pensacola, and led a force through the southern wilderness to Mobile. When the war ended, the mayor and the city council of Savannah declared their gratitude for his gallant service.[15]

MCINTOSH RETURNED to a family plantation, Fair Hope on the Sapelo River, and resumed his role as a leading businessman and planter in McIntosh County. He served as a ruling elder in the Darien Presbyterian Church.[16] When McIntosh died in 1826 he was buried in the family cemetery at Fair Hope.[17]

Two of McIntosh's sons carried on the family's military tradition. William Jackson McIntosh served as a lieutenant in the United States Navy; James Simmons McIntosh was wounded in the War of 1812 and received a mortal wound in 1847 while leading a brigade at Molino del Rey, Mexico.[18]

Samuel Elbert's grave in Savannah's Colonial Park

Chapter 9

Bodies in Motion

SAMUEL ELBERT AND JOHN MCINTOSH led active lives and after they died their remains remained active. Each of them was buried a first time and then was reburied.

Elbert and McIntosh were officers in the Georgia Continental line when they made a remarkable stand on the banks of Brier Creek. While other American soldiers fled in panic from a British bayonet charge, Colonel Elbert and Lieutenant Colonel McIntosh inspired their Georgia troops to stay and fight until almost all of them were killed, wounded or captured. Only then did Elbert and McIntosh surrender.

Elbert and McIntosh were held as prisoners of war until an officer exchange could be arranged with the British. Both of them returned to active duty.

After the American Revolution both Elbert and McIntosh established distinguished careers as civic leaders in the new nation.

IN 1788 SAMUEL ELBERT was buried in the family cemetery on "the Mount," an ancient Indian mound rising fifteen feet high and measuring fifty-five feet around, at Rae's Hall near Savannah.

Early in the twentieth century, the local public works department dug into the Mount to get fill dirt. The crew found a skull that they turned over to the Chatham County Commissioner's office; it subsequently disappeared.

Several years later, boys looking for Indian artifacts found bones sticking out of the trench cut by the public works department. Investigating further, the boys found coffin handles and nails, clues that the bones were not the result of an ancient Indian burial.

When the boys returned to the Mount another day, they discovered that someone had collected the bones, wrapped them in a handkerchief, and covered the package with Spanish moss.

Some of the boys took a few of the bones with them. After seeing a newspaper article headlined "Vandals Desecrate the Grave of General Elbert," two of the boys gave some bones to the Georgia Historical Society and another boy threw some bones into the trash.

Meanwhile, officers of the Georgia chapter of the Sons of the Revolution also removed bones from the Mount. After years of study, the officers concluded that the bones were the remains of General Elbert. A skeleton found near Elbert's remains was determined to be that of his wife, although skeptics harbored doubts.

The general's admirers planned a ceremonial reburial of the remains in Savannah's Colonial Park in 1924. Throngs gathered in a funeral cortege that marched down Liberty Street with a military escort while military guns in Forsythe Park thundered in salute.

Dignitaries gave speeches. The rector of Christ Church offered a prayer of invocation and another minister spoke a prayer of recommittal. A bugler played Taps as pall-bears placed a flag-draped casket containing bones believed to be the remains of Samuel Elbert into a granite tomb.[1]

IN 1826 JOHN MCINTOSH was buried in the family cemetery on a bluff beside the Sapelo River at Fair Hope in McIntosh County, Georgia.

Two decades later, a storm washed McIntosh's coffin out of the grave. The family reburied his body in a prestigious type of coffin that had not been invented at the time of his death. The new Fisk coffin was made out of iron and cost a hundred dollars, while a wooden coffin cost only a dollar at that time.

In 2006 a workman trimming bushes for a new owner of Fair Hope found the rusted iron coffin on the bank of the Sapelo River. Evidence proved that the coffin held the remains of John McIntosh. One clue was that the coffin was unusually long, and John was known to have been more than six feet tall, unusually tall for a man in the 1700s.

One of John McIntosh's descendants, Billy McIntosh of Savannah, arranged for John to be buried a third time, and this time farther from the river. John would be buried in the cemetery of another branch of the McIntosh family at Mallow, a plantation adjoining Fair Hope. Billy McIntosh scheduled the third burial of John McIntosh for October 23, 2010. *The Darien News* reported the event:

> On that beautiful October Saturday afternoon, a horse-drawn hearse carried "Col. John" only a mile between his first and second resting place at Fair Hope and what will hopefully be his last, at Mallow.
>
> The glass carriage arrived under a canopy of moss-draped oaks, kicking up dust, as the Savannah Pipe and Drum played "Going Home" on the bagpipes…

Beginning with Billy, the ceremonial shoveling of dirt into the grave began. In the Scottish tradition, flasks containing Scotch whisky were brought out, at which time swigs were taken prior to the pouring of the Scotch over the casket... [2]

The third burial of John McIntosh was a proud moment for his descendants, but it didn't exactly bring what Billy McIntosh's generation might call closure.

"The McIntoshes are so stubborn," Billy McIntosh told *The Darien News*. "He doesn't want to stay in the ground. This may not be the last!"[3]

Chapter 10

Reflections of Legends

THE LEGENDS associated with the Battle of Brier Creek contain elements common to world mythology, Celtic mythology, and the legends of King Arthur and his court. The following alphabetically arranged entries explore some of the common elements.

BATTLE: Many myths tell war stories, and Arthurian legend strings together one tale of combat after another.

"The battlefield is symbolic of the field of life," writes renowned mythologist Joseph Campbell, "where every creature lives on the death of another."[1] In an interview with Bill Moyers, Campbell says:

> During the Vietnam War, I remember seeing on the television young men in helicopters going out to rescue one or another of their companions, at great risk to themselves. They didn't have to rescue that greatly endangered young man. And so there I saw this same thing working, the same willingness of which Shopenhauer wrote, of sacrificing one's own life for another. Men sometimes confess they love war because it puts them in touch with the experience of being alive. In going to the office every day, you don't get that experience, but suddenly, in war, you are ripped back into being alive. Life is pain; life is suffering; and life is horror – but, by God, you are alive. Those young men in Vietnam were truly alive in braving death for their fellows.[2]

James Fergus was among the soldiers at Brier Creek who braved death for his fellows. As the soldiers fled the battlefield, Fergus paused to pull his fellows out of deep lagoons where they would have drowned without his help. After he built a raft and reached refuge on the South Carolina side of the Savannah River, he found a boat and returned several times to the dangerous Georgia side of the river to ferry his comrades to safety.[3]

Legends of Brier Creek contain the heightened dimensions of combat between kinsmen, the drama of last-second rescues of vanquished warriors, and the thirst for vengeance for a slain comrade.

CAPTIVITY: A warrior being taken captive, as Samuel Elbert was at Brier Creek, is a frequent element in the tales of King Arthur and his knights.

ESCAPE: James Fergus and the other lucky Americans who escaped through the swamps and across the river fit a common pattern in myth, legend and romance. The escape motif has some connection with nightmare, which the dreamer can escape from by waking up. One of the things that romance is about, writes Northrop Frye, "is the unending, irrational, absurd persistence of the human impulse to struggle, survive, and where possible escape."[4]

KINSHIP: The confrontation of Aeneas Mackintosh and John McIntosh at Brier Creek fits a mythological pattern. Joseph Campbell tells two legends that fit this pattern in *Creative Mythology*. In one legend, the Arthurian knight Parzival encountered his half-brother Feirefiz. Because their helmets covered their faces, they did not recognize one another:

> They rode immediately charging at each other, and each
> was amazed and angered when the other held his seat.

They battled fiercely and long. And I mourn for this; for they were two sons of one man. One could say that "they" were fighting if one wished to speak of two. They were, however, one. "My brother and I" is one body... One flesh, one blood, here battling from loyalty of heart, was doing itself much harm.[5]

After they called a truce, Parzival and Feirefiz removed their helmets, recognized one another as brothers, kissed and concluded peace. Feirefiz said, "You, my father, and I were one; but this appeared in three parts. I rode against myself and would gladly have killed myself."[6]

Later in the Parzival legend, an elder exclaims: "Alas, O World! You have slain your own flesh and blood. The Red Knight, Ither, was your relative." [7]

LAKES: The legend of a cannon lying at the bottom of Cannon Lake corresponds with archaeological evidence that Celtic peoples deposited many treasures, including spears and swords, in sacred lakes. The ancient Celts believed that lakes were holy places through which gods could be reached.[8] In Arthurian legend, the Lady of the Lake gives Arthur his sacred sword Excalibur and its scabbard; Morgan le Fay later throws the scabbard into deep water so that it is lost to Arthur forever.[9]

See also: RIVERS, WATER.

RIVERS: Maneuvers leading up to the Battle of Brier Creek involved crossing back and forth over the Savannah River and Brier Creek. Crossing a flowing stream is symbolic of passing a boundary or overcoming an obstacle to move from one realm or condition to another.[10]

In Arthurian tales, scholars write: "Rivers, as liminal spaces that both demarcate and lie between, often function as sites of contact or transition between the mundane world and the fantastical, between here and there."[11]

When the Arthurian knight Perceval crosses a flaming river, the great black horse that has carried him for miles disappears into the river.[12]

One of Arthur's most illustrious knights, the solar hero Sir Gawain, "arrived before a castle that lay beyond a broad, swift, navigable stream." A knight galloped up and challenged Gawain, who won the contest. A ferryman carried Gawain across the stream to the castle. "Gawain had now passed from the sphere of earthly adventure to a transcendental yonder shore."[13]

See also: LAKES, WATER.

THREEFOLD DEATH: Celtic mythology contains the concept of threefold death: dying in battle, drowning, and burning.[14] At Brier Creek, some men died in battle and some drowned trying to escape across the Savannah River. A second-hand account claims that some men died when the British burned the brush where they were hiding. For more on that second-hand account, see "Chapter 5: An Accusation of Atrocities."

WATER: Bodies of water – a swamp, a lake, a creek and a river – play crucial roles in the history and legend of the Battle of Brier Creek. Water is a pervasive element in mythology.

Arthurian legend is inseparable from water imagery:

> Even a cursory knowledge of Arthurian narrative confirms the importance of water, and land somehow bounded by water, to the Matter of Britain from its origins: Arthur's sword coming from and being returned to some mysterious watery realm, Lancelot and Gawain attempting to cross dangerous bridges into a kingdom that seems not quite mortal, the knights in numerous

texts who defend less-unearthly bridges as a point of honor.[15]

Water often has mythological meaning in the homeland of the Scottish Highlanders who fought at the Battle of Brier Creek. For more information see: *Folklore of Scottish Lochs and Springs* by James M. Macinlay, *Selected Highland Folktales* by R. Macdonald Robertson, and *The Folklore of the Scottish Highlands* by Anne Ross.

See also: LAKES, RIVERS.

PART THREE

A BIOGRAPHY

Starting as an orphan who inherited a lot in Savannah, Samuel Elbert became a prosperous merchant and planter, and married into a socially prominent family.

He served as one of Georgia's most accomplished officers throughout the American Revolution. Not long after the war ended, his fellow Georgians chose him to be their governor.

Chapter 11

Samuel Elbert

SAMUEL ELBERT WAS A SON of two of Georgia's earliest residents. His mother Sarah Greenfield was among the English settlers who founded Georgia in 1733. His father William Elbert emigrated from England to South Carolina as a young man and served as a ranger patrolling the region between the Combahee River and the Savannah River. When Georgia was founded, the rangers were stationed at Fort Argyle near Savannah to protect the new settlement. William and Sarah met at Argyle and married in 1734.[1]

William left the ranger service, encountered financial difficulties, and went to South Carolina for a year before returning to Georgia in 1737. William and Sarah had a daughter and a son, Samuel, who was born in Georgia in 1740. William became associated with the Malcontents who agitated against the policies of the Georgia Trustees, and left Georgia for good in 1742. The family settled in South Carolina at Euhaw, a short distance west of Beaufort. The Elberts became founding members of Euhaw Baptist Church, and William was licensed to preach in 1746.[2]

After Sarah died, William married Hannah Sealy in 1749. William bought three hundred acres at Purrysburg on the Savannah River in 1752 and became the owner of seven slaves. William died in 1754. By age fourteen, Samuel Elbert had lost his mother and his father. Samuel and his sister remained in South Carolina until Samuel inherited a lot in Savannah from a great-uncle and moved to Savannah in 1764.[3]

DURING THE DECADE preceding the American Revolution, Samuel Elbert established himself as one of the most successful merchants and traders in Savannah. He acquired large swaths of land and several slaves. In a development that would have implications at the Battle of Brier Creek, he became involved in the Indian trade and, since Augusta was the center of the Indian trade, became familiar with the territory along the Savannah River from Savannah to Augusta.

Elbert's social standing rose in 1769 when he married Elizabeth Rae, called "Betsy," whose father John Rae was a well-to-do planter and merchant. Samuel and Elizabeth lived on her family's riverfront plantation, Rae's Hall. Their marriage produced daughters named Sarah, Catherine, and Elizabeth, a son named Samuel Elbert, Jr., and three sons who died young.[4]

Like many men, both American and British, who would become officers in the eighteenth century, Elbert was a member of the Masons. Elbert established Unity Lodge No. 465 in Savannah and served from 1776 to 1786 as provincial grand master.[5]

Elbert showed interest in military matters when he organized a grenadier company in the Savannah militia and was commissioned captain in 1772. He traveled to England to study military theory. When he returned to Georgia, he put his learning to practical use as he drilled the grenadier company. On two occasions in 1774, Elbert and his grenadiers escorted Creek Indian delegates who traveled to Savannah for negotiations.[6]

AS THE REVOLUTION APPROACHED, Elbert was elected to serve on the Council of Safety in Savannah. His grenadier company complied with his allegiance to the patriot cause, and in August of 1775 Elbert led the company to Augusta to protect the town from loyalists. Five months later, as Georgia established a revolutionary government, Elbert took command of the state militia.

After the Continental Congress authorized Continental troops for Georgia, the Georgia Provincial Congress chose officers in January of 1776. The selections were made against a background of political factionalism. One faction was based in Christ Church Parish in the Savannah area and was considered to be conservative. A competing faction, considered to be radical, was based in St. John's Parish in the area around Midway and Sunbury.

The conservatives nominated Elbert to command the Continental troops. The radicals nominated Button Gwinnett of St. John's Parish. When Gwinnett won the election, the conservatives refused to accept the results. The impasse threatened to destroy the revolutionary government. At this point, both Gwinnett and Elbert withdrew from consideration, allowing the Provincial Congress to seek a compromise candidate.

The compromise candidate turned out to be Lachlan McIntosh, who was not affiliated with either faction and, as a resident of Darien, did not live in either faction's territory. As part of the compromise, Gwinnett was added to Georgia's delegation in the Continental Congress.

Elbert was placed in command of the 1st Battalion of the Georgia Continental line with the rank of lieutenant colonel. In July of 1776, Elbert was promoted to colonel and given command of the 2nd Battalion.[7]

In the early months of the war, British ships sailed up the Savannah River and landed troops on Hutchinson Island across the river from the town of Savannah. The British came to seize cargo boats loaded with rice, but the patriots had no way of knowing whether the British intended to capture Savannah and subdue Georgia. Elbert assisted McIntosh in defending Savannah from attack and driving off the British forces, although the British managed to haul off a few of the rice boats.

Throughout the war, Georgia faced threats from British forces in East Florida with headquarters in St. Augustine. In response, American forces attempted several times to invade East Florida and capture St. Augustine.

William Moultrie of South Carolina led the first attempted invasion in August and September of 1776. Each attempt failed, primarily due to stifling heat, raging tropical diseases and inadequate provisions.[8]

WHEN BUTTON GWINNETT returned to Georgia after his term in the Continental Congress, he resumed his campaign to become commander of the Georgia Continental forces. To displace McIntosh, Gwinnett began a smear campaign against the McIntosh family. The Gwinnett faction lodged complaints against McIntosh's older brother William, who was responsible for defending the Georgia-Florida border. William McIntosh removed himself from the controversy by requesting a leave of absence. Many of his officers also resigned in protest.[9] Lachlan McIntosh assigned Elbert to replace William McIntosh. "I flatter myself your taking the command at Altamaha will bring things to some order there," Lachlan told Elbert in January of 1777. "I am sure it will make me much easier & happier than I have been for some time."[10]

After smearing William McIntosh's reputation, Gwinnett accused the youngest McIntosh brother, George, of treason. Lachlan McIntosh was furious.

In February of 1777, Gwinnett was elected president of the Georgia Council of Safety, a position that gave him control of the state militia. Simultaneously with the George McIntosh controversy, Gwinnett made plans for an invasion of Florida without consulting Lachlan McIntosh. Unable to raise enough state militia for his expedition, Gwinnett finally asked McIntosh in late March for the support of Continental troops. Although McIntosh called the operation the "Don Quixote expedition to Augustine,"[11] he complied with Gwinnett's request. "Whatever my opinion of the expedition may be," McIntosh told his friend Henry Laurens, "I am resolved to go and do all in my power to forward it and bring it a happy issue."[12]

Before McIntosh left Savannah, Georgia forces led by Elbert reached Sunbury by the middle of April. Sickness took its toll just as it had the year before. Gwinnett ordered Elbert to launch the invasion, but Elbert insisted on taking orders from McIntosh rather than Gwinnett. "For God's sake let me hear from you immediately," Elbert wrote to McIntosh, "and if you think proper that I should proceed on the expedition, let me have your orders of directions as full as possible."[13]

When McIntosh arrived at Sunbury, he and Gwinnett argued for weeks over who should be in command of the expedition. The Council of Safety asked both of them to return to Savannah, leaving Elbert to lead the invasion. McIntosh agreed to turn the command over to Elbert "for peace' sake."[14]

McIntosh told Elbert, "I cheerfully resign the command of [the expedition] as it is to you, confident that everything will be done to serve our Country & the common cause that can reasonably be expected."[15]

Elbert loaded his men on transports escorted by two sloops and three row galleys and, on May 1, floated down the inland waterway from Sunbury toward Florida. Meanwhile, a mounted force under Colonel John Baker rode southward, planning to rendezvous with Elbert's men at the mouth of the St. John's River. The first obstacle facing Baker's men was the Altamaha River, which was in flood stage. When Baker's men finally got across the Altamaha, Indians attacked their camp and wounded two soldiers. Baker's men spent the rest of the day chasing the Indians without success. The next day they resumed their trek southward, where the spring-swollen Satilla and St. Mary's rivers awaited them. They managed to reach the rendezvous point according to schedule on May 12 and discovered that Elbert's flotilla had not yet arrived.[16]

Colonel Thomas Brown's Florida Rangers discovered the camp of Baker's invasion force on May 14. That night, Brown's Indian allies stole forty of Baker's horses. When morning came,

Baker followed the tracks for four miles and found the horses hobbled beside a swamp. Baker believed the Indians were waiting in ambush in the swamp. He left a party of men in plain sight to divert the Indians and sent two other parties to cut the hobbles and drive the horses away from the swamp. When Baker's tactic succeeded, the Indians came out of ambush and pursued the patriots for a mile. Although the patriots outnumbered the Indians sixty to fifteen, Baker could not make his men stop and face the Indians in battle. During the pursuit, a young Indian was killed and two of Baker's men were wounded. The Indians called off the chase and burned the woods so that they could not be tracked. Baker's men scalped and mutilated the dead Indian.[17]

Because the British knew the location of his camp, Baker moved inland. The British intercepted his line of march and prepared for battle. The British forces totaled about two hundred, while Baker had 150 to 180 horsemen. On May 17, Brown's loyalists and allied Indians ambushed the Americans at Thomas Creek, which flows into the Nassau River. The Americans attempted to retreat but were cut off by a hundred regular British soldiers commanded by James Mark Prevost. The Americans fled through the swamp, and Baker narrowly escaped capture. Three Americans were killed, nine wounded and thirty-one captured. As the Americans moved toward Georgia, one man drowned in the Satilla River.[18]

On May 18, Elbert's flotilla stopped at Amelia Island to gather provisions for the invasion force. Loyalists killed a lieutenant and badly wounded two men who were rounding up cattle and pigs. In retaliation, Elbert ordered that every house on Amelia be burned and all the livestock killed. Elbert's forces also seized at least seven slaves from plantations on Amelia.

While Elbert was at Amelia Island, fifteen of Baker's men arrived and told of their defeat. Three more of Baker's men arrived a few days later and reported that Indians had killed five of the Americans who had been taken prisoner in the battle at Thomas Creek.

Elbert attempted to continue the invasion down the inland waterway, but the flotilla was unable to navigate the narrow passage between Amelia Island and the mainland despite six days of effort. "Could we have got the galleys into St. John's River," Elbert said, "I would, with the men I have with me, made the whole Province of East Florida tumble."[19]

The invasion force had dwindled to about three hundred men healthy enough to fight and they became, Elbert reported, "very clamorous for want of provisions."[20]

When several men deserted from the American forces and joined the British forces, Elbert dreaded that "the Enemy will from them be informed of our strength and, what is worse, of our having had nothing but rice to eat for five days past."[21] Despite their hardships, Elbert said, "our brave fellows are in high spirits and wish an opportunity of a trial of skill with the Floridians, which I would have given them had I gone to the banks of St. John's River, did I not know too well the defenseless situation of the State to risk so many of the troops on the turn of a die."[22]

Because British forces guarded the river crossings and British vessels patrolled the coast, Elbert had no choice but to withdraw. Most of the force embarked on the flotilla to return northward, while a hundred men marched overland, destroying settlements and farms along the way.[23]

The famished men of Georgia's invasion force reached Fort Howe on the Altamaha River on June 9 and proceeded to Darien the next day. At Darien, Elbert ordered Colonel Screven of the 3rd Regiment to take several hundred men to the Satilla to protect Georgians who were driving cattle out of the disputed land. As soon as the Georgians succeeded in driving about a thousand cattle north of the Altamaha, Screven's regiment returned to Fort Howe.[24] While at Darien, Elbert received orders to return to Savannah.[25]

After returning to Savannah, Elbert asked Southern Department commander General Robert Howe to provide "good muskets and bayonets" for the Georgia Continentals. "It would make me happy," Elbert said. "The sorry trash I have at present being such a medley of rifles, old muskets & fowling pieces, with a few French traders, that I have no faith in them."[26]

Problems with Georgia's invasion of Florida damaged the prestige of the man who proposed the invasion, Button Gwinnett. When a new Georgia constitution called for a governor rather than a president as chief of state, Gwinnett ran for the post but was defeated. The assembly under the new constitution held hearings on Gwinnett's conduct during preparations for the invasion. As the hearings concluded, Lachlan McIntosh accosted Gwinnett. "You," McIntosh told Gwinnett, "are a scoundrel and lying rascal!"[27] Late in the evening of Thursday, May 15, McIntosh received a written challenge from Gwinnett. Because McIntosh had called him a scoundrel in public conversation, Gwinnett desired that McIntosh "would give satisfaction for it as a gentleman, before sunrise next morning in Sir James Wright's pasture, behind Colonel Martin's house."[28] McIntosh answered that he would meet Gwinnett with a pair of dueling pistols. He agreed to arrive at Wright's pasture before sunrise, "although the hour is rather earlier than my usual."[29] On the dueling ground, Gwinnett and McIntosh wounded one another in the thigh. Gwinnett's wound became infected and he died three days later. McIntosh recovered in about three weeks.[30]

DURING THE SUMMER of 1777 in coastal Georgia, many of the soldiers became ill, so General McIntosh moved most of them inland to healthier locations with better water, leaving a detachment at Sunbury. "The 2nd Regiment, Colonel Elbert, is ordered up Savannah River," wrote McIntosh, "and send such attachment as may be necessary outside the settlements upon the branches of that river." Elbert's order book shows that he was stationed at

Augusta from August 13 to September 11, adding to his familiarity of the terrain in which the campaign culminating in the Battle of Brier Creek would be conducted less than two years later.[31]

While Elbert was stationed at Augusta, the Georgia government tried to go over McIntosh's head by giving Elbert command of the Continental troops on the western frontier; in making the announcement, Governor John Treutlen described Elbert as "a courageous, active and brave commander."[32] Elbert felt "obliged to decline" because "while General McIntosh contends for the command of the Continental Troops in the State, and I continue to hold my commission, I am bound to obey him." If the politicians felt that his decision was harmful to the state, he told them, he was willing to resign from the military and resume "the character of a citizen."[33]

As controversy continued to swirl around McIntosh, his old friend and business partner Henry Laurens came to his aid. Laurens, who held a powerful position in the Continental Congress, arranged for McIntosh to report to General George Washington for reassignment. McIntosh ordered on October 10, 1777, that "the command of the Continental forces in this state devolves till further orders upon Colonel Elbert, and the army and its dependents are ordered to respect and obey him as their commanding officer."[34]

Five days later, Elbert appealed to General Howe for "three or four handy brass field pieces properly mounted with the necessary apparatus, adding thereto some round & canister shot to fit them. I find on inquiry that we have not a ream of cartridge paper in the State, if of that article any is to be procured please likewise order us some, as I would willingly have a quantity of musket cartridges ready in case of emergency; at present we have none."[35]

DESPITE THEIR EARLIER FAILURES, American military leaders planned yet another invasion of East Florida in 1778. The plan called for coordination among Georgia state troops, the Georgia navy, Continental troops from the Georgia line, Continental troops from South Carolina's 1st Regiment, 3rd Regiment and 6th Regiment, South Carolina militia, and Continental troops from the Southern Department.

The Georgia Continentals marched southward to the Altamaha River and arrived on April 14 at the ruins of Fort Howe, where they planned to rendezvous with the other bodies of troops.[36]

On April 16, Elbert led about 350 Georgia troops to Darien. The infantry went aboard three galleys, and an artillery detachment loaded two field pieces on a flatboat. The flotilla went down the Altamaha to St. Simon's Island. Elbert "earnestly entreated" his officers and soldiers "to pay the strictest attention to their duty, in which case their commanding officer will insure them of success against the plunderers of their country and the common enemies of the rights of mankind."[37] While a few marines remained on the galleys, the infantry went ashore. A detachment of one hundred men entered the town of Frederica and captured several members of a British naval crew.

Early on the morning of April 19, the American galleys took aim at the enemy ships *Hitchinbrook*, *Rebecca* and *Snow*. Elbert reported to General Howe "our three little men-of-war made an attack on these three British vessels, who have spread terror on our coast, and who were drawn up in the order of battle; but the weight of our metal soon dampened their courage." After the *Hitchinbrook* and *Rebecca* ran aground and laid over at low tide, their captains "struck the British tyrant's colors and surrendered to American arms." The British sailors "took to their boats and abandoned everything on board, of which we immediately took possession. Captain Ellis, of the *Hitchinbrook*, was drowned and Captain Mowbrary, of the *Rebecca*, made his escape."[38]

Cargo on the captured ships included uniforms for South Carolina Continental troops; the uniforms previously had been captured by the British in naval action off Charleston. Elbert's victory deprived the British of control of the inland waterway and reduced British East Florida's naval force to only a single frigate.[39]

The Americans secured the captured ships at Sunbury and then made a forced march back to Fort Howe, where Elbert expected a British attack. "I know your anxiety for the safety of this state is such that no time will be lost," Elbert told Colonel John White. Elbert also asked White to arrange for rice and salt to be shipped from the coast to Fort Howe.[40]

On May 9, General Howe reached the fort on the Altamaha named in his honor.[41] Howe was delighted that Elbert had launched the campaign with a victory, and declared "how highly he approves the conduct of Colo. Elbert in the late expedition against the enemy at Frederica, and with equal pleasure applauds the spirited behavior of the officers and men, both of the galleys and of the army who were upon that command."[42]

While the Americans remained in camp, Howe approved the execution of several deserters. "Desertion is of all other crimes the greatest a soldier can be guilty of," Howe told his men. "In committing it every moral sanction is violated; the cause of freedom, the darling rights and privileges—both of the present and succeeding generations—which soldiers were ordained particular to secure and protect, are relinquished and betrayed."[43]

In late May the army moved from Fort Howe to Reid's Bluff on the south side of the Altamaha, and in early June proceeded into contested territory. By June 22, Howe's command had reached the south side of the Satilla River and by the end of June the army camped at the ruins of Fort Tonyn on the St. Mary's River. Illness struck hundreds of soldiers, who were sent to hospitals on the Georgia coast. The soldiers remaining in camp lacked an adequate amount of tents, kettles, canteens, medicine, food and equipment.[44]

While Howe commanded the Georgia Continentals and several units of South Carolina Continentals, Georgia Governor John Houstoun maintained command of a force of Georgia militia. On June 30, a detachment of Georgia militia attacked a band of East Florida Rangers near a British outpost at Alligator Creek Bridge; more than twelve Georgians were killed and several were wounded; one British soldier was killed, and several British and loyalist soldiers were wounded.[45]

Conditions continued to deteriorate in Howe's camp. Because provisions were resupplied sporadically, the men ran out of rice and went for three days without bread.[46] On July 14, about two months after he arrived on the Georgia-Florida frontier, Howe called off the expedition. He praised the "the cheerfulness with which the men supported a long and fatiguing march under a variety of unavoidable yet distressing circumstances."[47]

Elbert directed an evacuation at Cumberland Island. "The whole of the troops are to be embarked by low water," Elbert ordered on July 17, "that the fleet may be ready to sail with the first of the flood."[48] By July 28, Elbert was in Savannah.

The 1778 invasion of East Florida, like the previous attempts, had ended ignominiously. The most significant consequence was that Georgia forces were so weakened that they were vulnerable to British attack.

WHEN INDIANS ALLIED with the British threatened Georgia's western frontier in August of 1778, Elbert sent the 1st Battalion to protect backcountry residents. Troops "in Savannah must be sent to Augusta immediately," Elbert ordered, and "the remainder who are to the southward marched after them." As an act of "self-preservation," Elbert authorized Georgia soldiers who were prisoners of war on parole "to be armed for the purpose of securing helpless & innocent women and children from the scalping knife."[49] A week later, Elbert transferred the Light Dragoons from Ebenezer to Augusta. In October, Elbert instructed two companies of light infantry from the 3rd and 4th Battalions "to march immediately to Augusta," accompanied by four pieces of artillery.[50]

While dealing with the threat on the western frontier, Elbert also planned defenses against an invasion from the south. "As it is expected that a very considerable army will be employed in this State in a little time," Elbert ordered deputy commissaries "to have magazines of every species of provisions stored at Savannah, Sunbury and Augusta... A large quantity of barreled pork and wheat flour will be particularly wanted, which can't be done without."[51]

IN THE AUTUMN OF 1778, a British force under Lieutenant Colonel James Mark Prevost marched from East Florida toward Georgia by land, and a force under Lieutenant Colonel L.V. Fuser sailed up the waterway. Not knowing that the British came primarily to gather provisions, Elbert prepared to defend Georgia against an all-out invasion. Elbert marched southward from Savannah and set up a command post at the Great Ogeechee crossing. He fortified the position and awaited the British invaders.[52]

Colonel Prevost entered Georgia on November 19, destroying plantations, confiscating property, and taking all able-bodied men prisoner. Local militia skirmished with Prevost at Bulltown Swamp and at Riceboro Bridge but could not stop his advance toward Elbert's position.

Colonel John White marched about a hundred men with two pieces of artillery to intercept Prevost at Midway. White's men hurriedly constructed a breastwork across the road. When General James Screven with twenty militiamen joined White at Midway, the combined force relocated to a stronger defensive position a mile and a half below Midway. Soon afterward, the British force under Colonel Prevost arrived and a battle began. During the fighting, General Screven suffered a fatal wound.

When Colonel Prevost's horse was shot from under him, the Americans thought they would win the battle, but Prevost mounted another horse and continued to press the attack. White retreated several miles past Midway.

A British scouting party sent to Sunbury reported to Prevost that Colonel Fuser's force had not yet arrived. Prevost, considering his own lack of reinforcements and White's prospect of reinforcements from Elbert, decided to return to St. Augustine. On the way back, Prevost's men burned the church known as the Midway Meeting House and burned all homes and barns in the area. The men plundered the plantations and took all the valuable items they could carry.

Fuser's ships had been delayed by storms. While Prevost's unit was leaving Midway, Fuser's foot soldiers were disembarking near Sunbury. As the infantry marched toward Sunbury, the ships sailed to positions where they could shell Fort Morris. Inside the fort, Lieutenant Colonel John McIntosh commanded 127 Continental troops as well as some militia and local volunteers. When Fuser demanded that the Americans surrender Fort Morris, McIntosh replied, "Come and take it."[53] Fuser maintained the siege while awaiting reports of Colonel Prevost's activities. When Fuser learned that Prevost was returning to St. Augustine, he called off the siege and sailed back to Florida. Georgia's safety, however, was short-lived. In December a British expeditionary force arrived at Savannah.

ELBERT'S ROLES in the first Battle of Savannah, the Battle of Brier Creek, and the Siege of Yorktown are described in the first four chapters of this book. While at Yorktown, Elbert became friends with the Marquis de Lafayette, and later named a son Emanuel de LaFayette Elbert.[54]

AS THE WAR CAME TO AN END, Continental officials recognized Elbert's service by promoting him to brigadier general in 1783, and Georgia honored him with the highest rank in the state militia: major general. Elbert also served as vice president of the Georgia chapter of the Society of Cincinnati, an organization of former officers in the Continental Army.

When Elbert returned to Georgia, he worked to rebuild his mercantile business in Savannah and to restore his plantation on the Savannah River. He also established a distinguished career as a civic leader in the new nation. In the year the war ended, he was chosen to be the surveyor of Chatham County and became a vestryman at Christ Church. He continued to serve as grand master of the Masonic Order in Georgia. Always interested in Indian affairs, he participated in treaty negotiations held at Augusta. He was selected as a delegate to Congress in 1784, but decided to stay home.[55]

"In July, 1785, by an almost unanimous vote, [Elbert] was elected governor of Georgia," wrote Georgia historian Charles C. Jones, Jr. "In the discharge of his duties of this high station he manifested the same ability, energy, diligence, good judgment, decision of character and exalted manhood which had characterized him in other positions."[56] Another Georgia historian, William Berrien Burroughs, wrote that Elbert's "administration was clean, energetic and businesslike and was marked by the passage of the bill creating the State University."[57] Although the university was chartered during Elbert's administration, the University of Georgia did not open until sixteen years later.[58]

While governor, Elbert got rid of a few dozen "banditti" who were marauding in the same area of South Georgia where Elbert had struggled to maintain order during the Revolution. Elbert asked the Liberty County Militia, supported by volunteers from Savannah, to "take the most effectual means to secure the villains who are at this time assembled between the Satilla and St. Mary's Rivers, with a number of negroes, horses & other property supposed to have been stolen from the citizens."[59]

Three months later, Elbert told Colonel John Baker of Sunbury, "I have information of a gang of plunderers between St. Mary's and St. John's who have connections in this state, which makes it necessary to have something immediately done to prevent their becoming more formidable. I therefore wish to renew my former orders to you to detach a party if possible to make short work with them."[60] At the same time, Elbert authorized a magistrate on Cumberland Island "to take such measures as will effectually rid you of the rest of the villains who infest your part of the state."[61]

Elbert maneuvered to protect Georgia's interests when Congress negotiated treaties with Creek and Cherokee tribes. He received reports from leaders of the Cherokee Nation "with an open heart which I always had for my friends & Brothers, the Cherokees, ever since we took each other by the hand in Augusta."[62]

Reports of abuse appalled him. "It is a pity that the people on our frontiers will behave so cruelly towards those poor Savages;" Elbert wrote, "not content with having their lands, but to rob, beat and abuse them likewise, is enough to bring down divine vengeance on their heads." He worried that "the blood of some poor women & children, who might suffer in consequence of such conduct, will undoubtedly lay at their doors." He asked "every good citizen to make severe example of such notorious offenders."[63]

AFTER HIS TERM as governor expired, Elbert served in the General Assembly. He was elected in December of 1787 as sheriff of Chatham County, a prestigious position in eighteenth century Georgia; he retired due to ill health in September of 1788.[64]

Elbert died at age 48 on November 6, 1788. "His death was announced by the discharge of minute guns, and the colours of Fort Wayne and the vessels in the harbor being displayed half-mast high," reported *The Georgia Gazette*. "In private life he was among the first to promote useful and benevolent societies. As a Christian he bore his painful illness with patience and firmness, and looked forward to his great change with an awful and fixed hope of future happiness. As a most affectionate husband and parent, his widow and six children have great cause to lament his end, and society in general to regret the loss of a valuable member. His remains were attended on Sunday to Christ Church by the Ancient Society of Masons (of which he as the past Grand Master in this state), with the members of the Cincinnati as mourners accompanied by a great number of his fellow citizens whom the Rev. Mr. Lindsay addressed in a short but well adapted discourse on the solemn occasion. Minute guns were fired during the funeral, and every other honour was paid his memory by a respectable military procession composed of the artillery and other military companies."[65]

gators guard the realm
of flowing creek and river
surrounded by swamp

PART FOUR

REVOLUTIONARY WAR SITES

Alex Lee (seated) presides at a Remember Brier Creek memorial service in Sylvania in 2016, the 237th anniversary of the Battle of Brier Creek during the American Revolution

Chapter 12

Remember Brier Creek

TWO CENTURIES ELAPSED between the day American soldiers lost a battle at Brier Creek Battleground and the day their heirs placed a monument on the battleground. The most plausible explanation for the delay is that people seldom celebrate defeat. But they remember.

The earliest documented effort to commemorate the battleground occurred in 1917, when residents of Sylvania invited William Harden, the editor of *Georgia Historical Quarterly,* and Otis Ashmore, a vice president of the Georgia Historical Society, to discuss the importance of preserving local history. Harden reported that he and Ashmore "were cordially received, and found the people much interested, many of them expressing a desire to assist in the work." Ashmore delivered an address on the Battle of Brier Creek. After dinner, the group took an automobile tour of "the points named in connection with the Battle of Brier Creek."[1]

In the 1920s a bill was introduced in Congress to authorize a memorial at the battleground. Thirty-one women in Screven County organized the Brier Creek Chapter of the Daughters of the American Revolution (DAR) in 1921 and received a charter in 1923. In 1939 the Brier Creek DAR declared that the battleground should be recognized. The DAR reported in 1940 that a historical marker was placed beside Burtons Ferry Highway, which crosses Brier Creek upstream of the battleground, and a monument to the patriots who died at Brier Creek was placed in the DAR park in Sylvania.

In 1954 the Georgia Free and Accepted Masons placed a marker at Brannen's Bridge on Brier Creek in honor of General Samuel Elbert, who was a Mason and who was taken prisoner at Brier Creek. In 1956 local historian Clyde Hollingsworth assisted the Historic Georgia Foundation with the design and placement of a historical marker at Brannen's Bridge; the marker includes a map that Hollingsworth identified while doing research in Washington D.C.

Attempts to gain recognition from the National Park Service and the Georgia Historic Sites Division were unsuccessful. One reason given for the lack of interest in the site is that the patriots lost the battle and the American public does not tend to celebrate defeats.[2]

Around the turn of the millennium, local historian Alex Lee spurred a new effort to commemorate the battle and recognize the battleground. He was a founding member of the Remember Brier Creek Committee along with Jason Beard, Dr. A.L. Freeland, the Rev. David Buie, Caroline Pope, Norm Hill and Margaret Evans, who was the mayor of Sylvania at the time. The Sylvania city manager also serves on the committee; Crawford Carter was succeeded by Stacy Mathis. Sylvania's Comprehensive Plan subsequently included the Brier Creek Battleground as a city project. The Georgia Society of the Sons of the American Revolution (SAR) and ExploreGeorgia.org published a pamphlet on the Battle of Brier Creek as part of a series, "Georgia's Revolutionary War Trail," that is distributed at visitor information centers; Lee, a member of the Mill Creek Chapter, wrote the pamphlet and Bill Ramsaur, a member of the Marshes of Glynn Chapter, edited it.

The City of Sylvania received a federal grant through the Georgia Department of Transportation for $100,000 matched with $25,000 in city money to pay for research defining the battlefield and locating the graves of patriot soldiers; historical documents indicate that 150 Americans were buried on or near the battlefield. The City of Sylvania contracted with Daniel Battle, a conflict archaeologist who operates Cypress Cultural Consultants of Beaufort, South Carolina, to conduct the research. In 2014 he submitted "Locating the Forgotten Revolutionary War Battle of Brier Creek (9SN254); Metal Detector Survey, Burial Search, and Extensive Archival Research." After concluding his contractual relationship with the City of Sylvania, researcher Daniel Battle has gone off in his own direction. He has publicized the Brier Creek Battleground through a Facebook account and has given presentations to the Sons of the American Revolution and other organizations including the Southern Campaigns of the American Revolution. When the Brier Creek chapter of the Georgia Society of Sons of the American Revolution received its charter on November 19, 2016, Battle became the chapter's vice president; Craig Wildi was the founding president and twenty-one men were charter members.[3] The next year Battle transferred his membership to the South Carolina Society of Sons of the American Revolution.[4]

In November of 2015 the Remember Brier Creek Committee and the City of Sylvania sponsored a Battle of Brier Creek Design Charrette with students and faculty from the University of Georgia College of Environment and Design. After receiving input from state and local public officials and local historians, the students presented conceptual designs for a battlefield park in the Tuckahoe Wildlife Management Area, a monument to the patriots who are buried at Brier Creek, programs to encourage visitation, and a website to promote appreciation of the battleground. Those proposals are in the early stages of implementation.[5]

The Remember Brier Creek Committee established an account through the City of Sylvania to help pay for the monument and related projects. The Sylvania and Screven County local governments allocated funding for the monument and asked for funding from the state government.[6]

Early in 2016, the Georgia Department of Natural Resources (DNR) granted permission to use five hundred acres in the Tuckahoe Wildlife Management Area for an interpretive trail and approved the location of a monument. Late in 2016, DNR announced that a design for a visitors' center is being considered.[7]

In the autumn of 2016, the Georgia Historical Records Council presented a Local History Advocacy Award to Alex Lee in recognition of his work with the Remember Brier Creek Committee and other research projects.[8]

The Remember Brier Creek Committee held an event in February of 2017 to commemorate the 238th anniversary of the Battle of Brier Creek. State Senator Jesse Stone announced that the state legislature had put $150,000 in the budget for a battlefield memorial. "I'm excited about the future of the Battle of Brier Creek," Stone told the committee. "News about Brier Creek will be heard all over Georgia and be told to all the people in the South."[9]

In April, the Department of Natural Resources announced $100,000 in funding for the battlefield monument, bringing the total to $250,000.[10]

Three months later, Senator Stone arranged a meeting in Sylvania with the Remember Brier Committee, representatives of the Department of Natural Resources (DNR), the Daughters of the American Revolution, the Sons of the American Revolution, county and city officials, and State Representative John Burns. DNR officials announced that a battlefield monument had been designed using input from the University of Georgia Charrette. A construction timetable had been approved to have the monument in place by the 239th anniversary of the battle. The perseverance of Alex Lee and the Remember Brier Creek Committee had been rewarded. Referring to the 1917 visit by officers of the Georgia Historical Society, Lee said, "This is one hundred years since the beginning of efforts to recognize the Brier Creek Battleground."[11]

Chapter 13

Come See Us

ONE DAY IN 1996 ALEX LEE came to my office and said something like, "I can show you where the Battle of Brier Creek was fought."

I said something like, "What Battle of Brier Creek?"

Lee is a pharmacist and local historian in Screven County, Georgia. I was the editor of the county newspaper, The Sylvania Telephone, at the time.

Lee drove me out to the battleground about ten miles from Sylvania. He explained that the battle was a significant event in American history and the site could be a tourist destination because it is on public property in the Tuckahoe Wildlife Management Area. After we walked around the battlefield, he drove me along back roads skirting the Savannah River and showed me other historic sites, telling stories of local history the whole time. I was amazed, and still am, at his breadth and depth of knowledge. One of his stories was about British Captain Aeneas Mackintosh rescuing his distant kinsman Continental Colonel John McIntosh; that story caught my attention since I already was researching the Mackintosh clan and the McIntosh family because I have ancestors from McIntosh County, Georgia.

I wrote a story headlined "Battle site rarely gets recognition" with the lead sentence "If the Brier Creek Battleground receives the recognition it deserves, says local historian Alex Lee, Screven County will benefit from the publicity."[1]

A few months after Lee showed me the battlefield, I moved across the Savannah River to Allendale, South Carolina, and edited the newspapers in Allendale and Barnwell. Then I got out of the newspaper business; I call myself a recovering journalist. As a community citizen without the constraints of journalistic objectivity, I became involved in efforts to promote heritage tourism in the Allendale region. Since the Brier Creek Battleground lies between Allendale and Sylvania, I thought that promoting the site would help the local economies in both Allendale County and Screven County. In 2012 I self-published a thin booklet about the Battle of Brier Creek. Later I published *Brier Creek Battleground* with more comprehensive historical information, maps and a selection of color photographs. After the efforts of Lee and his fellow members of the Remember Brier Creek Committee led to the installation of a monument at the battleground, I decided to write an updated book; this is it.

Promoting heritage tourism to stimulate the local economy continues to be among my goals. I hope you will visit the Brier Creek Battleground and related sites along the Savannah River, and I hope you will eat a meal or spend a night in the area. I also hope you will obtain a Georgia hunting or fishing license or Lands Pass, which you can download at *GoOutdoorsGeorgia.com* or purchase from local stores that sell sporting goods; it's a good value as the price of admission to the battleground and it also helps support land, water and wildlife conservation.

Main Street Sylvania has made plans to paint a mural of the Battle of Brier Creek on the side of a downtown building.

Sylvania is a charming small town with restaurants, antiques shops, an outdoor outfitter and other stores, including Possum Eddy Hardware, which is named after an oxbow lake in the Tuckahoe Wildlife Management Area. The Soda Shop Gallery at 105 South Main Street offers work by local crafters, artists and authors, including me.

Lodging

Kinchley Place Bed and Breakfast at 309 Singleton Avenue, Sylvania, GA 30467, is an elegant Victorian house passed down through generations of a Sylvania family.

The Sylvania Inn at 404 W. Ogeechee St. is a basic but up-to-date motel in the center of town.

Several old motels remain from the era when U.S. Highway 301 was a bustling tourist corridor.

If you prefer rustic accommodations, Leaning Pine Campground and RV Resort at 3637 Old River Road rents cabins as well as full RV hook-ups, drive-through campsites and tent camping sites with amenities; despite its Sylvania address, Leaning Pine is near the Savannah River miles away from any town; it is closer than eight miles from the Brier Creek Battleground, but because of dirt roads the travel time is about fourteen minutes.

Travel Information

For the City of Sylvania, go to CityofSylvaniaGeorgia.com

For the Screven County Chamber of Commerce, go to ScrevenCounty.com

To access the official state tourism website, called *About Georgia*, go to ExploreGeorgia.org

More information is available online and in a printed brochure titled "Battle of Brier Creek, March 3, 1779: Brier Creek was the pivotal encounter which re-established Georgia as a Royal Colony." The brochure is part of a series titled Georgia's Revolutionary War Trail: Discovering Our Heritage and History published by the Georgia Society Sons of the American Revolution and ExploreGeorgia.org. The URL is www.grwt.gassar.org

A map of the Tuckahoe Wildlife Management Area, home of the Brier Creek Battleground, is available free online from the Hunting Maps (Region 3) page of the Georgia Department of

Natural Resources Wildlife Resources Division site on the web at http://www.georgiawildlife.com/maps/hunting/region3

Driving Directions

The Brier Creek Battleground nestles in a rural area of Screven County connected by a web of dirt roads, narrow paved roads, Georgia Highway 24 and U.S. Highway 301. If you map out your route on the internet, print a copy of the map and carry it with you because cell phone service can be spotty in and around the Savannah River swamp. I have some suggestions based on my personal preferences, but they are not the only routes and not necessarily the best routes. As Bob Dylan sings, don't say I didn't warn you if your train gets lost.

The following driving directions start from towns in the seven counties served by the Lower Savannah River Alliance, a nonprofit organization that promotes nature-based tourism. Visitors from farther away can make their way to one of these towns and then follow the directions. Visitors from Augusta, for example, can go to Waynesboro, while visitors from Savannah can go to Springfield.

FROM SYLVANIA, GEORGIA (ABOUT 10 MILES)

Take East Ogeechee Street 5.5 miles, cross Georgia Highway 24 onto County Road 243 (Brannens Bridge Road), go 4.5 miles, and cross Brier Creek on three bridges. The boat landing with the historical markers will be on your left and the road to the battlefield in Tuckahoe Wildlife Management Area will be slightly farther on your right.

FROM WAYNESBORO, GEORGIA (ABOUT 40 MILES)

Option 1: The simplest route follows Georgia Highway 24 from Waynesboro about 36 miles to Brannens Bridge Road. Turn left on Brannens Bridge Road, go 4.5 miles, and cross Brier Creek on three bridges. The boat landing with the historical markers will be on your left and Main Road in Tuckahoe Wildlife Management Area will be slightly farther on your right.

Option 2: If you like leisurely drives through scenic countryside, take Georgia Highway 24 out of Waynesboro, turn left on Thompson Bridge Road, bear right onto Georgia Highway 23 and proceed to Girard. From Girard, you have several options.

Option 2A: If you want to follow the approximate route that the British troops took to the Battle of Brier Creek, take Millhaven Road from Girard to Millhaven. The site of Paris's Mill where the British army crossed Brier Creek on the way to the Battle of Brier Creek is marked by Georgia Historical Marker 124-4, "British Army Crossing." From Millhaven, follow Plantation Road to U.S. Highway 301. Continue straight across U.S. Highway 301 onto Pine Grove Inn Road. Follow Pine Grove Inn Road for 8.2 miles to a sharp turn to the right, where the name of the road becomes Brannens Bridge Road; follow the curve to the right and proceed on Brannens Bridge Road to the Brannens Bridge boat landing at Brier Creek.

Option 2B: If you leave Girard by first bearing left on Stoney Bluff Road, next bearing right on Oglethorpe Trail, and then proceeding to U.S. Highway 301, you have at least two options. One option is to cross Highway 301 and proceed on Old River Road to Pine Grove Inn Road. Turn left and follow Pine Grove Inn Road until it becomes Brannens Bridge Road. Follow Brannens Bridge Road to the boat landing on Brier Creek. This route has advantages and disadvantages. An advantage is that Old River Road dates back to the Colonial era and you will be following essentially the same route that Revolutionary War soldiers followed. Because Old River Road is not paved, the disadvantages are that the trip is bumpy at best and becomes treacherous in wet weather.

Option 2C: Another option from the intersection of Oglethorpe Trail and U.S. Highway 301 offers a more reliable route, especially in wet weather. Turn right (south) from Oglethorpe Trail onto U.S. Highway 301 and then turn left onto Pine Grove Road, continue onto Brannens Bridge Road and go to the boat landing on Brier Creek.

FROM SPRINGFIELD, GEORGIA (ABOUT 43 MILES)

Take Georgia Highway 21 northwest about 20 miles to Newington. Turn right onto Georgia Highway 24 and go about 18 miles. Turn right on Brannens Bridge Road, go 4.5 miles, and cross Brier Creek on three bridges. The boat landing with the historical markers will be on your left and Main Road in Tuckahoe Wildlife Management Area will be slightly farther on your right.

Adventurous travelers might want to explore the back roads along the Savannah River and get onto Georgia Highway 24 east of Newington.

FROM ALLENDALE, S.C. (ABOUT 29 MILES)

Take U.S. Highway 301 South across the Savannah River, about 14 miles.

From the Georgia Visitor Information Center, which will be on your right near the foot of the Savannah River Bridge, proceed south on Highway 301 for about 5.2 miles.

Turn left onto Pine Grove Inn Road for 8.2 miles to a sharp turn to the right, where the name of the road becomes Brannens Bridge Road; follow the curve to the right and proceed on Brannens Bridge Road to the Brannens Bridge boat landing at Brier Creek.

FROM BARNWELL, S.C. (ABOUT 42 MILES)

Take S.C. Highway 3 eastward and go about 21 miles. Turn right (south) on U.S. Highway 301 and follow Highway 301 about six miles across the Savannah River.

From the Georgia Visitor Information Center, which will be on your right near the foot of the Savannah River Bridge, proceed south on Highway 301 for about 5.2 miles.

Turn left onto Pine Grove Inn Road for 8.2 miles to a sharp turn to the right, where the name of the road becomes Brannens Bridge Road; follow the curve to the right and proceed on Brannens Bridge Road to the Brannens Bridge boat landing at Brier Creek.

FROM ESTILL, S.C. (ABOUT 42 MILES)

Take S.C. Highway 3 westward and go about 21 miles. Turn left (south) on U.S. Highway 301 and follow Highway 301 about six miles across the Savannah River.

From the Georgia Visitor Information Center, which will be on your right near the foot of the Savannah River Bridge, proceed south on Highway 301 for about 5.2 miles.

Turn left onto Pine Grove Inn Road for 8.2 miles to a sharp turn to the right, where the name of the road becomes Brannens Bridge Road; follow the curve to the right and proceed on Brannens Bridge Road to the Brannens Bridge boat landing at Brier Creek.

FROM HARDEEVILLE, S. C. (ABOUT 78 MILES)

Take U.S. Highway 321 northward about 36 miles to Estill. Follow the directions from Estill given above.

Daniel McDonald Johnson
July 4, 2018

A sign marks the entrance to the battlefield memorial

Chapter 14

The Brier Creek Battleground

THE SITE OF THE BATTLE OF BRIER CREEK is on public property in the Tuckahoe Wildlife Management Area administered by the Georgia Department of Natural Resources. Of the 15,100 acres in Tuckahoe, a portion covering 2,521 acres has been designated as the Brier Creek Battleground and has been nominated for inclusion in the National Register of Historic Places. Depending on your interests and your timetable, you could spend anywhere from hours to years exploring Tuckahoe by vehicle, on foot, on horseback or by canoe, kayak or small boat. In addition to its historic and prehistoric sites, Tuckahoe offers opportunities to observe wildlife, including rare species, and to view splendid landscapes and waterscapes.

The public park beside Brier Creek at Brannen's Bridge provides historical markers

If you have limited time, two stops should be sufficient. The first is a public park beside Brannens Bridge Road about 4.5 miles east of Georgia Highway 24. A nearby landmark is the Georgia Department of Natural Resources office at 6199 Brannens Bridge Rd., Sylvania, GA 30467; phone (912) 564-7878. The GPS coordinates for the DNR office are: N32.811 W81.466. The GPS coordinates for the Brannen's Bridge boat landing and picnic area are: 32.810430, -81.484298. If you drive across the three bridges spanning the swamp, you can appreciate the immense obstacle the swamp presented to the soldiers who fought in the Battle of Brier Creek. At the park, you can stand at the edge of the main channel of Brier Creek, and you can peer into the creek swamp. Next to the green-roofed picnic shed stands Georgia Historical Marker 124-20, "Battle of Brier Creek - Mar. 3, 1779." The Grand Lodge of Georgia Free and Accepted Masons erected another marker, "General Samuel Elbert."

The memorial at the Brier Creek Battleground features Georgia marble and the landscaping features native plants

Your second stop should be the battleground memorial. To get there from the Brannen's Bridge park, turn left out of the driveway of onto Brannens Bridge Road, go about a tenth of a mile, and turn right onto a gravel road. A sign at the entrance says "Tuckahoe Wildlife Management Area / Battle of Brier Creek Revolutionary War Memorial." A short distance down the road, another sign says "One of the following is required to enter this property (age 16 or older): License to hunt or fish; Lands Pass (not valid to hunt or fish); You can purchase these at GoOutdoorsGeorgia.com, or 1-800-366-2661."

As you proceed down the gravel road you will see the memorial in the V-shaped intersection of Cannon Lake Road and Main Road. A nearby wildlife clearing provides spacious parking. The site is considered not only historic but also sacred because American patriots are buried on or near the battleground. State and local law enforcement officers protect the site against removal of artifacts or other acts of vandalism.

The memorial consists of a Georgia granite wall and earthen berms enclosing a meandering crushed-granite path lined with signs that offer insight into the significance of the battle. The monument area is planted in native grasses, small trees, and woody shrubs. "Creating a location in the landscape specifically devoted to the Battle of Brier Creek provides a place for visitors to pay their respect and an educational opportunity to learn of the great stand and sacrifice made by the American soldiers in one battle that brought each of us freedom," says a planning document published by the Georgia Department of Natural Resources. The document points out that "the natural landscape and plant species are quilted into a naturalized memorial landscape. Weaving the natural and constructed edges into a seamless designed landscape of natural aesthetics and minimal maintenance is ideal to respect the quality of the land and the memory of the battle." The "enclosure concept" of the granite wall and earthen berms is intended to evoke emotional responses from visitors.[1]

Margaret Evans, a founding member of the Remember Brier Creek Committee and a former mayor of Sylvania, speaks at the dedication of the battlefield memorial on March 3, 2018

TWO HUNDRED PEOPLE attended the dedication of the battleground memorial, organized by DNR and the Georgia Society Sons of the American Revolution (SAR), on March 3, 2018, the 239th anniversary of the battle. SAR provided a color guard to present and retire the American flag and re-enactors to fire volleys with flintlocks and a cannon. Several chapters of the National Society of the Daughters of the American Revolution presented commemorative wreaths, as did representatives of state, county and city governments.

The dedication of the monument was "indeed a dream come true," observed Margaret Evans, a former mayor of Sylvania and a charter member of the Remember Brier Creek Committee.

Dr. David D. Crass, director of DNR's Historic Preservation Division, thanked Evans for her leadership, noting that she "carried the flag through this whole process." A visit to Brier Creek,

Crass said, "has a rare power – the power to transport us back in time to an awful moment when that kid from the North Carolina swamps confronted one of the mightiest armies the world has ever seen. There are hundreds of those stories out there, just waiting to be told."[2]

Betsy Sternau and her family traveled from Illinois to attend the dedication. They came in honor of her ancestor Samuel Elbert, the Georgia commander who made a brave stand at Brier Creek until being wounded and taken prisoner. "I want my children to feel the personal connection I feel to Brier Creek," she said. Sternau called the memorial "a place where anyone can now walk in the footsteps of our ancestors, visualize the events of March 3, 1779, reflect and honor those who fought and those who still lie buried in unmarked graves, surrounded by the beauty of Brier Creek."[3]

The organizers of the dedication ceremony plan to hold commemorative events at the memorial each year on the first Saturday in March.

Sons of the American Revolution fire a salute in honor of the dedication of the memorial at the Brier Creek Battlefield

SHORTLY AFTER the Brier Creek Memorial was dedicated, the Brier Creek Revolutionary War Battlefield Association formed to encourage the preservation of the battlefield and to interpret local history through exhibits and programs. Stephen Hammond, Sonny Pittman, Tommy Christopher, State Senator Jesse Stone, John Fitzner and Homer "Chip" Durden served as officers. Dr. Al Freeland, a charter member of the Remember Brier Creek Committee, became a member of the board of directors of the Brier Creek Revolutionary War Battlefield Association along with Grace Waits, Dr. John Derden, Alicia Evans, Wilder Smith Jr., Scotty Scott, Dianne Fitzner, Dess Smith III, Lee Smith, J. Michael Tomme, and Betsy Sternua, who is a descendant of Brier Creek hero Samuel Elbert. Interested persons may apply for membership.[4]

THE GEORGIA NATIONAL Register Review Board has nominated the Brier Creek Battlefield to the National Register of Historic Places "as the location of one of the most influential American Revolutionary War battles that occurred in Georgia." The proposed historic district, which contains fourteen archaeological sites, covers 2,521 acres in the Tuckahoe Wildlife Management Area and 165 acres of adjoining private property. "The property's integrity of location and association are evidenced by historic documentation along with the recovery of military artifacts during archaeological studies," the nomination proposal says, "while the open pine forest, bordering cypress swamps, and the battlefield's overall rural character effectively portray integrity of setting and feeling."[5]

The park at Brannen's Bridge provides a boat landing

Chapter 15

Paddle to the battle

Experienced, skillful, resourceful boaters may want to explore the confluence of Brier Creek and the Savannah River. Experienced boaters know that rivers and creeks are wild things, offering both beauty and danger.

A few of the dangers, in addition to drowning and hypothermia, are snakes, wasp nests, alligators, strong currents and hidden snags. Even if the river does not on its own cause a problem, it complicates health emergencies because you can't get to an emergency room, and emergency medical responders can't get to you, without much time and trouble.

Among numerous boat landings on the Savannah River are one at Burton's Ferry on U.S. Highway 301 and another at Cohen's Bluff (historic Matthews Bluff) off S.C. Highway 3.

There are boat landings on Brier Creek at Brannens Bridge Road and at U.S. Highway 301. Many of the oxbow lakes in the Tuckahoe Wildlife Management Area have primitive ramps or canoe throw-ins.

Online maps are available through the Georgia Department of Natural Resources.

One of the boat landings in the Tuckahoe Wildlife Management Area is at Possum Eddy

Chapter 16

Along the Savannah River

THESE REVOLUTIONARY WAR SITES in South Carolina and Georgia are listed in geographical order going from downstream to upstream along the Savannah River.

A tour boat berths at River Street in historic Savannah

SAVANNAH

Savannah was founded in 1733 and served as the capital of Georgia during the Colonial and Revolutionary eras. British forces led by Archibald Campbell captured Savannah in December of 1778. French and American forces tried to wrest control of

Savannah from the British in 1779 but were repulsed in some of the bloodiest fighting of the entire War of the American Revolution. For visitor information, see the *Visit Savannah* website.

When the British captured Savannah, they took control of "an excellent barracks fit to contain a thousand soldiers," reported Archibald Campbell, who went on to claim "there is room for two thousand more men in the houses of the town without distressing the inhabitants."[1]

Campbell gave a thorough description of Savannah in his journal:

> At break of day I reconnoitered the environs of Savannah, and found that the town occupied the summit of a plain or table land, which was not less than 50 feet above the level of the river. That the buildings were regular, and formed an oblong square of 700 yards in length along the river, and 400 yards in breadth towards the country. That an area of 200 yards ranged along the front of the town between the buildings and the bluff, which had been dressed in a regular slope towards the river.
>
> On the bluff, at the distance of 400 yards from the south end of the town, the Fort of Savannah stood; from which fort the ground fell suddenly into the rice swamps to the westward.
>
> From the south side of the town, the country had a gentle fall towards the new barracks, which were at the distance of 400 yards. A high wood bounded this side of the plain in a line with the new barracks, bending towards the town as it approached the Augusta Road on the west, and the road to Tatnel's on the east. From the south end of the town, the country fell gradually to the village of Yamacraw, and from thence more suddenly into the swamps to the west-

ward of Savannah. In short, one side of the town was secured by the river, the two ends were shut up by the rice swamps, and the fourth side was encircled by an extensive wood of lofty pines, the whole very capable of being fortified with advantage.[2]

A Swiss cross marks the historic settlement of Purrysburg

PURRYSBURG

The site of Purrysburg, where General Benjamin Lincoln established headquarters at the time of the Battle of Brier Creek, is beside the Savannah River near Hardeeville in Jasper County, South Carolina. From U.S. Highway 321 in Hardeeville, take Church Street until it ends at Purrysburg Road, turn right (north) on Purrysburg Road and watch for South Carolina Historical Marker 27-3 on your left near the intersection with Honey Hill Road. GPS Coordinates: 32° 18.344' N, 81° 7.209' W

The Huguenot Society of South Carolina erected a monument in the shape of a Swiss cross in the 1940s. The cross is at the end of a small lane between riverfront homes near the state historical marker.

"A lonely, cross-shaped monument of stone on the banks of the Savannah River marks the site of Purrysburg, an early Swiss settlement that eventually failed," says a 2016 posting on the

Jasper County Chamber of Commerce website. "In 1731, the King of England granted land on the Savannah River to Swiss colonizer Jean Pierre Purry. Hundreds of German-speaking and French-speaking Swiss colonists arrived with the dream of establishing a silk trade in the new colony. But malaria and other hardships proved fatal to the European colonists, and the settlement died a slow death. Purrysburg lingered on at least until the time of the American Revolution, serving as the first headquarters of the American army under General Benjamin Lincoln. Today, the river landing and the cemetery at Purrysburg are still in use, and several fine, new homes are being built near the site."[3]

The grave of Georgia's first constitutional governor, John Adam Treutlen, rests near Jerusalem Lutheran Church at Ebenezer

EBENEZER

Historic Ebenezer in Effingham County, Georgia, was one in a string of fortified positions along the Savannah River established by Archibald Campbell after capturing Savannah. The New Ebenezer Retreat is located at 2887 Ebenezer Road, Rincon, GA 31326. A living history museum at Ebenezer is located at 2980 Ebenezer Road, Rincon, Georgia 31326; office phone: 912-754-7001.

The historic site provides spectacular views of the Savannah River. Revolutionary-era sites at Ebenezer include Jerusalem Lutheran Church, which was established in 1733; construction of the building began in 1767 and was completed in 1769. Ruins of Revolutionary War redoubts and Colonial-era roads are visible at Historic Ebenezer. Graves of soldiers and civilians who died during the American Revolution have been located through research conducted by Dan Elliott with the support of the Georgia Salzburger Society. For more information go to the *Visit Ebenezer* website.

Ebenezer Creek, the only coastal stream designated as a Wild and Scenic River by the Georgia General Assembly, provides paddlers in canoes or kayaks with several leisurely day trips through a wondrous blackwater stream ecosystem. A public boat landing with free parking and restroom facilities provides access to Ebenezer Creek at 980 Long Bridge Road, Rincon, GA 31326.

Campbell described Ebenezer and other fortified posts in his journal:

> Cherokee Hill is eight miles from Savannah and may of consequence be applied as an intermediary post to support the communication of the great western road and to secure a cross tract to Ogichee, which enters the great road at this station...
>
> Abercorne is by the road about 9 miles from Savannah, upon the side of a creek, which communicates with the great river, and by which our provisions are happily conveyed and carted from thence to Ebenezer...
>
> Zubly's Ferry is twenty-three miles from the town of Savannah. At this station, the great road

communicates to Purisburg over a long tract of low swamps cut by two considerable creeks, over which the rebels had wooden bridges that are now broken up. The ground on our side of the swamp has from its height an excellent command of this road...

Ebenezer is distant twenty-five miles from the town of Savannah and situated on the bank of the great river between two considerable swamps. As those swamps are only passable over the two wooden bridges, it requires a very great detour for troops to turn them. Here I am constructing some redoubts to shut up the gorge between the two swamps, and I mean to establish this post as the advance magazine for the army. Ebenezer from its happy situation above the town of Purisburg makes it a post of consequence so long as General Lincoln with the Carolina army, consisting of five thousand men, continues to encamp in the neighborhood [at Purrysburg on the South Carolina side of the river]. The 1st and 2nd Battalions of the 71st Regiment have charge of Ebenezer.[4]

When Campbell went to Augusta, he took the 1st Battalion of the 71st Regiment with him and left the 2nd Battalion of the 71st Regiment along with a troop of dragoons "and others to make 800" rank and file soldiers at Ebenezer. Campbell's expedition to Augusta set out from Ebenezer at daybreak on January 24, 1779.[5]

TWO SISTERS FERRY

Continental General Benjamin Lincoln set up camp briefly at Sisters Ferry, in the vicinity of the present B&C Landing off Sand Hills Road in Jasper County, South Carolina. The ferry landing on the Georgia side of the river is on private property near Clyo in Effingham County.

Georgia founder James Oglethorpe ordered the ferry to be established by 1740, and operations continued, with occasional interruptions, until 1921.[6]

British engineer John Wilson recorded "From Ebenezer to Trytland's [a plantation owned by John Adam Treutlen] or the Two Sisters is ten miles, after passing the creek, which you cross upon quitting Ebenezer, you come to a few good plantations that extend from the right of the road almost to the riverside; they yield both corn and rice and have plenty of pasture for cattle; the bank of the river here at Trytland's is higher upon this side than the other, and the ferry (which is sometimes used) a little above the house is very difficult to be got to, in the manner of that at Zubilee's."[7]

British Colonel Archibald Campbell stationed the New York Volunteers and Light Infantry and a troop of rifle dragoons at Two Sisters with orders to patrol the countryside within fifteen miles of their post. "The Two Sisters is thirty-five miles from the Town of Savannah," Campbell wrote, "and the ground on this side has a very excellent command over the road which leads across the swamp to the ferry."[8]

A stairway from the picnic area to the boat landing reveals the height of the bluff at Tuckasee King

TUCKASEE KING

Effingham County operates a park with picnic areas, restrooms and a boat landing at Tuckasee King, site of an ancient Indian town.

The Savannah River crossing from Tuckasee King in Georgia to Palachacola in South Carolina was strategically important in the Colonial era.

"From Two Sisters to Tuccasse-king is 3 miles," observed British engineer John Wilson during the American Revolution. "This last plantation lies high in comparison to the ground that we have just traveled over; the present possessor has but a scanty livelihood if his stock of cattle does not turn out to good account; a run of water that washes the bottom of a gulley which separates the rising ground that this farm house stands upon from a higher hill of deep sandy ascent makes this situation more convenient; there is no scarcity of cattle or hogs and great plenty of venison in this district."[9]

HUDSON'S FERRY

Newington in Screven County, Georgia, is the nearest present-day town to the location of historic Hudson's Ferry. The exact location of Hudson's Ferry is on private property overlooking the Savannah River. Working in the 1980s, historians Robert Scott Davis and Arthur Gross determined the location of Robert Hudson's house, saw mill, cowpen and ferry. The nearby landmark that they noted in *Encounters on a March through Georgia* was Blue Springs Methodist Church, which is at the intersection of Georgia Highway 24 and Blue Springs Road.[10]

A corps of discovery organized by the Southern Campaigns of the American Revolution fellowship in 2016 traveled along Coursey Landing Road to get as near the site of Hudson's Ferry as possible without trespassing on private property.[11]

The house at Hudson's Ferry was "forted in by palisades"[12] by 1775. "From Tuccassee-king to Hudson's house and ferry is 10 miles; the road... is very good and easy," an engineer in the 71st Regiment observed shortly before the Battle of Brier Creek. "The bank of the river on this side is high and steep, almost parallel to the main road and nowhere above 2 miles distant from it: Mount Pleasant, Killicrankie, &ca. upon the right hand are well improved plantations, valuable for their produce and immediate communication with the river; this stage has few swamps near the roads and the woody part is an open firm pine barren that may be easily galloped through."[13]

The engineer continued, "Hudson's house is upon a high healthy open situation and close to the bank of the river which overlooks a field and swampy wood upon the Carolina side. The flat used at the ferry was stationed a little above the house; to quit this ground you descend gradually an easy piece of road, cross a run of water that once kept a mill agoing, and then raise a hill that is steep for carriages and difficult to be forced if disputed by an enemy."[14]

On the return leg of an expedition from Savannah to Augusta in February of 1779, Archibald Campbell told his engineer "to prepare materials for shutting up the White House at Hudson's Ferry with a stockade redoubt, so as to secure it against any sudden attack."[15]

While Campbell was at Hudson's Ferry, he turned over command of his troops to James Mark Prevost. Two weeks later Prevost set out from Hudson's Ferry to attack the American camp at Brier Creek.

Cannon Lake Road ends at site of Miller Bridge

MILLER BRIDGE

At the time of Archibald Campbell's Savannah-to-Augusta expedition, River Road crossed Brier Creek on "the lower old bridge." The bridge is often called the Miller Bridge or the

Freeman-Miller Bridge because Richard Miller owned the land to the north of the bridge and John Freeman owned the land to the south. Settlers operated a ferry at the site in the early 1760s and built the bridge by the late 1760s.[16]

The site of the bridge is at the end of present-day Cannon Lake Road in the Tuckahoe Wildlife Management Area. The road gets its name from stories that a cannon fell off the bridge and subsequent legends that the cannon remains on the bottom of an oxbow lake that connects to Brier Creek at the site of the Miller Bridge.

John Wilson, an engineer on Campbell's expedition, describes the approach to "the lower old bridge" from what he called Mill Creek, present-day Buck Creek. "From this place to the beginning to the causeway that carries you to the bridge, you pass in a pine barren [and then] through an ugly swamp that covers a piece of the road with water. The causeway is more than 800 yards long with a deep swamp immediately upon either side; the quantity of water that is constantly here made it necessary for the preservation of the causeway to open a passage across the road over which a bridge is made which you pass before you get to the main bridge upon the creek, which you no sooner pass than you get to a farm with a few out houses." Wilson mentioned two "small plantations" within four miles of the bridge.[17]

Campbell observed, "Briar Creek is about 100 feet wide at the bridge, and about eight or ten feet in depth; the current of the water is slow, and the bottom muddy." Campbell fortified the settlement at Brier Creek by building a barrier of sharpened tree trunks and branches around "such houses as were pierced with loopholes, so as to make a tolerable resistance against musketry."[18]

When Campbell returned from Augusta, he took a different route than the one he had taken on his way to Augusta. The American army that attempted to pursue Campbell, however, followed River Road. When the Americans reached Brier Creek, they discovered that someone had burned the Miller Bridge. The Americans encamped at the site of the bridge for two days before relocating on higher ground a mile upstream of the bridge. The Battle of Brier Creek took place at the second encampment.

Cohen's Bluff overlooks Savannah River near Matthews Bluff

MATTHEWS BLUFF

Continental General John Ashe and other survivors of the Battle of Brier Creek took refuge at General Rutherford's headquarters at Matthews Bluff. The historic site is in the vicinity of Cohen's Bluff boat landing in Allendale County, South Carolina.

To visit Cohen's Bluff/Matthews Bluff from the Georgia Visitor Information Center, take U.S. Highway 301 north across the bridge. The former South Carolina welcome center (now the Lower Savannah River Alliance Nature Center) will be on the right.

A mile and a half past the former welcome center, turn right (east, toward Estill) on River Road /S.C. Highway 3. Travel 9.1 miles to Cohens Bluff Road. (NOTE: Along the way, you will pass two historic sites, Erwinton Plantation and Antioch Christian Church.)

Turn right off S.C. Highway 3 onto Cohens Bluff Road, and proceed to the public boat landing on the Savannah River. GPS Coordinates: Latitude 32.84223, Longitude -81.42657

Historical records from the 1750s mention residents of the Matthews Bluff area, confirming it as one of the first settlements in present-day Allendale County.[19] The settlers may have used an old Indian path that followed the Coosawhatchie River and branched off to the Savannah River at Matthews Bluff. The settlers raised cattle, produced timber products, and planted enough crops for themselves and their livestock. A Baptist meetinghouse was the only social institution at Matthews Bluff in the Colonial era.[20]

During the American Revolution, the Pipe Creek Company of Light Horse guarded Matthews Bluff as a strategically important location.[21] In maneuvers preceding the Battle of Brier Creek, the Americans sent Major John Grimke's South Carolina artillery and General Rutherford's North Carolina regiment of seven hundred infantry to Matthews Bluff. The plan called for them to cross the river and to march three miles to General Ashe's camp, but Ashe did not complete a road through the swamp from his camp to the river in time for the plan to work.

British forces attacked Ashe's camp on March 3, 1779. Most of the Americans fled within five minutes of the attack. When he realized the battle was lost, Ashe followed them. Because the confluence of the Savannah River and Brier Creek hemmed them in, the fleeing men slogged through the swamps and tried to cross the river on log rafts. Between fifty and one hundred men drowned. The luckier ones spent the night hiding in a canebrake on the South Carolina side of the river. Ashe crossed the river in a rowboat and found refuge at Matthews Bluff.[22]

Ten months after the Battle of Brier Creek, a skirmish was fought at Matthews Bluff. In December of 1780, the British sent an expedition of forty-five soldiers down the South Carolina side of the river to eliminate American posts that were disrupting the passage of supply boats from Savannah to British garrisons at Augusta and Ninety Six. At Matthews Bluff, the expedition encountered an American force under Captain James McCoy and Captain Johnston. Because the Americans occupied a superior position, they were able to kill the British commander, Lieutenant Kemp, and fifteen of his men.

The British sent reinforcements from Augusta, and the Americans drew reinforcements from the adjacent district. In mid-January of 1781, the Americans, now commanded by Colonel William Harden, launched a nighttime attack on the British camp at Wiggins Hill. The local militiamen serving with the British fled, but the regular soldiers held their ground. After sunrise, Harden attacked again. The British counterattacked and drove off the Americans. Seven Americans were killed and eleven wounded; at least seven men serving with the British were killed. The site of the Wiggins Hill battleground is a matter for speculation, although the local history book *Allendale on the Savannah* suggests that the site is near the former South Carolina welcome center on U.S. Highway 301.[23]

Colonel Harden withdrew to an island in the Coosawhatchie Swamp, where sympathetic local residents cared for his wounded men. A neighboring loyalist captured one of the residents and tried to force him to reveal the location of the wounded soldiers; when the resident refused to betray the men, the loyalist murdered him. After that, conflict between patriot and loyalist neighbors raged. Loyalists hanged nearly a dozen patriots, including a sixteen-year-old boy. Partisans tortured a man to death, murdered seventeen residents of a neighborhood upstream of

Burton's Ferry, burned homes, and stripped women and children of their clothing.[24]

After the American Revolution, Matthews Bluff retained its importance to transportation along the Savannah River. Travelers from Savannah to Augusta had the option of taking the steamboat *Carolina* as far as Purrysburg, dining on the boat, and continuing the trip by horse-drawn coaches. According to an advertisement, the passengers were entrusted to "sober, excellent drivers, with able and gentle horses, chaise lighted with overhead kerosene lanterns."[25] The coaches stopped at Matthews Bluff to change horses; the passengers ate breakfast during the break.[26] The first steamboat on the Savannah River began operating in 1808. A decade later, seven steamboats followed regular schedules to and from Savannah and Augusta. Between 1820 and 1865, seventy steamboats were launched on the Savannah River; thirteen of them caught fire, six exploded, and seven sank. During the Civil War, Savannah River traffic was stopped. Some boats were confiscated, others were burned. Captain John G. Garnett beached *The Swan* and set it afire rather than surrender it to the Union. It was only partly burned; after the war, he rebuilt it and resumed operations on the Savannah River until 1873. At least five other steamboats owned by South Carolinians were still on the river in the period following the war. During this period, two Cohen brothers built a store and warehouse to the north of Matthews Bluff. Competition from railroads eventually put steamboats out of business. By 1870, only *The Ross* and *The Katie* followed regular schedules up and down the Savannah. In World War II, the only two boats navigating the river were pressed into coastal war service.[27]

Ethel Rouse, who grew up six miles from the river on Matthews Bluff Road, now called Bluff Road, wrote down her memories of life in the steamboat era. She could hear the music from *The Katie*'s steam calliope long before the boat appeared around the bend. The music served as a signal for passengers and freight-handlers to be prepared when the boat docked. Local farmers shipped their cotton, lumber, seed, and other produce by steamboat, and obtained their fertilizer and other goods.

In her time, one steamboat company used the landing at Matthews Bluff and a rival company operated its landing about a mile northward at Cohen's Bluff. Area residents – both black and white – would crowd around the landings to meet the boats on Wednesdays and on Saturday nights. Cohen's Bluff was more popular with young people, who enjoyed picnics with wonderful food and cold lemonade, thanks to ice brought up from Savannah by boat. The teenagers and adults spent the day dancing in the warehouse. The captains often would take the local people for a short voyage, and the dancing would continue on board the boat. Red velvet draperies curtained off sections of the upper deck. Colored glass reflected brilliant hues. In one section, berths were arranged for ladies and children; another section was for men. Passengers could play games and enjoy entertainment, or could simply enjoy the scenery. The captain presided over meals, which were well prepared and graciously served.[28]

People still enjoy the tradition of picnicking at Cohen's Bluff. Recreational boaters use the public landing to launch their craft into the Savannah River. Anglers walk along the banks of the river searching for the perfect fishing spot. Birdwatchers and sightseers stroll across the wooded bluff and enjoy scenic overlooks across the water. For a history buff, the bluff is the stuff that dreams are made of.

A boat landing is available on the Georgia side of the Savannah River at Burton's Ferry

BURTON'S FERRY

The most significant crossing place on the Savannah River near the Brier Creek battleground is Burton's Ferry. At the time of the Battle of Brier Creek, the American supply train was placed at Burton's Ferry, eight miles away from the American encampment at Brier Creek.

The U.S. Highway 301 Bridge over the Savannah River marks the location of historic Burton's Ferry. A nearby landmark is the Georgia Visitor Information Center at 8463 Burton's Ferry Highway, Sylvania, GA 30467; phone (912) 829-3331. The GPS coordinates are: 32.935717, -81.516860

Across the highway from the Georgia Visitor Information Center, a historical marker discusses Burton's Ferry. A paved road beside the historical marker leads to a boat landing on the Savannah River.

PARIS'S MILL (sometimes spelled Parris Mills)

Paris's Mill, the place where the British crossed Brier Creek in a maneuver to trap the Americans, is now known as Millhaven. The site is marked by Georgia Historical Marker 124-4, "British Army Crossing," at Brier Creek Bridge in Millhaven, 3 miles NW of Georgia 24.

Water flowing over a dam provided power for a mill operated by Francis Paris. On their way to the Battle of Brier Creek, British troops dismantled Paris's house for materials to build a bridge; British officials later reimbursed Paris for his loss.[29]

A monument capped with a Celtic cross marks the location of the Revolutionary-era fort in Augusta

AUGUSTA

Augusta occupied a key strategic location during the American Revolution. Shortly after Archibald Campbell led British troops in the capture of Savannah, Campbell set out in January of

1779 on an expedition to occupy Augusta. After he withdrew from Augusta in February, American forces pursued him as far as Brier Creek, setting the stage for the Battle of Brier Creek.

St. Paul's Episcopal Church at Sixth and Reynolds streets (605 Reynolds Street, Augusta, GA 30901) occupies the location of a fort constructed in the Colonial era. When Campbell occupied Augusta, he strengthened the defenses of the fort and garrisoned it with a "chosen company of Florida Rangers."[30]

"St. Paul's Episcopal Church is located on the banks of the Savannah River, where in 1735, General Oglethorpe founded Georgia's second city as a fortress and Indian trading center upriver from Savannah," says the Augusta Convention & Visitors Bureau website. "The church grounds are the site of the first church of Augusta built in 1749 and the location of old Fort Augusta built by colonists as protection against Indians. Rebuilt as Fort Cornwallis during the Revolutionary War, the fort was captured by 'Lighthorse Harry' Lee, which was a great blow to the British cause... The cemetery dates from the very earliest days of the church and has existing tombstones dating from as early as the 1780s. It is the resting place of a number of important people. At the rear of the churchyard is a Celtic cross of granite erected by the Colonial Dames on the site of Fort Augusta/Cornwallis. General Oglethorpe brought the damaged cannon at its foot from England in 1733 for use at the fort."[31]

In his journal entry for February 1, 1779, Archibald Campbell gives this description:

> Augusta consisted of a number of straggling houses arranged in a long street lying parallel to the river at the distance of 100 yards. The great road leading from the lower country entered the south end of town at right angles to this street and, after passing it, extended to the ferry, which goes across to South Carolina.

The Savannah River was not less than 200 yards in breadth, 10 feet deep, and the stream moderately quick.

The plain to the southward of the ferry road extended four miles in length and terminated in a swamp at the bend of the river a little below Moore's Bluff.

> [NOTE: Moore's Bluff on the South Carolina side of the river is the site of an Indian village called Savannah Town that was known to colonists as early as 1685. Colonists built Fort Moore on the strategically located river bluff in 1716 to protect Indian trading routes. Soldiers garrisoned Fort Moore until 1766, when the establishment of Augusta across the river made it unnecessary. A South Carolina Historical Marker for Savannah Town and Fort Moore is on Sandbar Ferry Road (State Highway 28) in the Aiken County town of Beech Island. GPS coordinates: 33.43931666, -81.91011666.]

To the northward of the ferry road, the plain was about two miles in length, and terminated in a ravine, from whence the country began to rise gradually. From the Savannah River, this plain was about 3 miles in breadth, one thousand yards of which from the banks of the river had been cleared of wood and tolerably well cultivated.

From the ferry road, Alligator Pond of about 80 feet in breadth and 10 feet in depth, extended one mile and a half in a parallel direction with the river at the distance of one thousand yards; from the side of which pond, a small rill of water with deep banks emptied itself into the river; on the south side of which rill, close to the bank of the river, stood a church, and about half way from this rill to the ravine at the upper extremity, Fort Grierson, a stockade work with four bastions and eight small pieces of cannon had been erected, about 60 yards from the west side of the principal street.[32]

"Upon coming near Augusta different roads lead to the town and enter it at as many places," wrote an engineer accompanying Campbell. "Within some miles of the town there are three or 4 mills and plenty of Indian corn; the upper country yields plenty of wheat and several inhabitants distill whiskey from wheat &c. which will, upon a pinch, and in an emergency, satisfy a soldier in place of rum."[33]

Notes

Notes to Chapter 1:
The Capture of Savannah, December 1778

[1] Gordon Burns Smith, *Morningstars of Liberty: The Revolutionary War in Georgia 1775-1783* (Milledgeville, Georgia: Boyd Publishing, 2006), 2:19.

[2] Charles C. Jones, *The Life and Service of the Honorable Major General Samuel Elbert of Georgia*, (1887, Charleston, S.C.: BiblioLife, 2011), 21.

[3] Archibald Campbell, *Journal of an Expedition against the Rebels of Georgia in North America under the Orders of Archibald Campbell Esquire Lieut. Colol. of His Majesty's 71st Regimt. 1778*, ed. Colin Campbell (Augusta, Georgia: Richmond County Historical Society, 1981), 7.

[4] Campbell, *Journal of an Expedition,* 103, n. 12

[5] Campbell, *Journal of an Expedition,* 21.

[6] Campbell, *Journal of an Expedition,* 23-26.

[7] Alexander A. Lawrence, "General Robert Howe and the British Capture of Savannah in 1778," *Georgia Historical Quarterly* 36: 4 (December 1952), 311.

[8] Lawrence, "General Robert Howe and the British Capture of Savannah," 316, 320-21.

[9] Campbell, *Journal of an Expedition,* 28.

[10] Lawrence, "General Robert Howe and the British Capture of Savannah," 324-25; Campbell, *Journal of an Expedition,* 43-44.

[11] Campbell, *Journal of an Expedition,* 36-37.

[12] Campbell, *Journal of an Expedition,* 40.

[13] Campbell, *Journal of an Expedition,* 102, n. 5.

Notes to Chapter 2:
The March to Augusta, January-February 1779

[1] Archibald Campbell, *Journal of an Expedition against the Rebels of Georgia in North America under the Orders of Archibald Campbell Esquire Lieut. Colol. of His Majesty's 71st Regimt. 1778*, ed. Colin Campbell (Augusta, Georgia: Richmond County Historical Society, 1981), 48-49.

[2] David S. Heidler, "The American Defeat at Briar Creek, 3 March 1779," *Georgia Historical Quarterly* 66.3 (Fall 1982), 318.

[3] Edward J. Cashin Jr. and Heard Robertson, *Augusta and the American Revolution: Events in the Georgia Back Country, 1773-1783* (Augusta, Georgia: Richmond County Historical Society, 1975), 26.

[4] Campbell, *Journal of an Expedition*, 49-50, 108 n. 45.

[5] Campbell, *Journal of an Expedition*, 50-52.

[6] Campbell, *Journal of an Expedition*, 53.

[7] Campbell, *Journal of an Expedition*, 54.

[8] Campbell, *Journal of an Expedition*, 54, 120 n. 136.

[9] Campbell, *Journal of an Expedition*, 57-58.

[10] Campbell, *Journal of an Expedition*, 62-68.

[11] Campbell, *Journal of an Expedition*, 68.

[12] Campbell, *Journal of an Expedition*, 70.

[13] Campbell, *Journal of an Expedition*, 74-75.

Notes to Chapter 3:
The Battle of Brier Creek: March 3, 1779

[1] "Order Book of Samuel Elliott, Colonel and Brigadier General in the Continental Army, October 1776 to November 1778," *Collections of the Georgia Historical Society Vol. V, Part 2* (Savannah: The Morning News Print, 1902), 11.

[2] Davis S. Heidler, "The American Defeat at Briar Creek, 3 March 1779," *Georgia Historical Quarterly* 66.3 (Fall 1982), 322; Joshua B. Howard, "'Things here wear a melancholy appearance:' The American Defeat at Briar Creek," *Georgia Historical Quarterly* 88.4 (Winter 2004), 486, 490.

[3] John C. Dann, *The Revolution Remembered: Eyewitness accounts of the War for Independence* (Chicago: University of Chicago Press, 1980), 177.

[4] Heidler, "The American Defeat at Briar Creek," 322-23.

[5] Dann, *The Revolution Remembered,* 177; Heidler, "The American Defeat at Briar Creek," 324-25.

[6] Heidler, "The American Defeat at Briar Creek," 323.

[7] Heidler, "The American Defeat at Briar Creek," 325; William Moultrie, *Memoirs of the American Revolution*, (New York: The New York Times & Arno Press, 1968), 1: 341; David K. Wilson, *The Southern Strategy: Britain's Conquest of South Carolina and Georgia, 1775-1780* (Columbia: University of South Carolina Press, 2005), 94.

[8] William Gordon, *The history of the rise, progress, and establishment, of the independence of the United States of America: including an account of the late war* (London: printed for the author, 1788), 3:233; Frank Moore, *Diary of the American Revolution from Newspapers and Original Documents* (New York: The New York Times & Arno Press, 1969), 2: 141 n.

[9] Heidler, "The American Defeat at Briar Creek," 325; Wilson, *The Southern Strategy,* 94.

[10] Heidler, "The American Defeat at Briar Creek," 328; Wilson, *The Southern Strategy*, 98-99; Moultrie, *Memoirs*, 1: 340-42.

[11] Heidler, "The American Defeat at Briar Creek," 328-29; Wilson, *The Southern Strategy*, 96; Dann, *The Revolution Remembered*, 179.

[12] Dann, *The Revolution Remembered*, 179.

[13] Heidler, "The American Defeat at Briar Creek," 328-29.

[14] Archibald Campbell, *Journal of an Expedition against the Rebels of Georgia in North America under the Orders of Archibald Campbell Esquire Lieut. Colol. of His Majesty's 71st Regimt. 1778*, ed. Colin Campbell (Augusta, Georgia: Richmond County Historical Society, 1981), 77.

[15] Wilson, *The Southern Strategy*, 96.

[16] Dann, *The Revolution Remembered*, 181.

[17] Moultrie, Memoirs, 1: 324-25.

[18] Dann, *The Revolution Remembered*, 181.

[19] Moultrie, *Memoirs*, 1: 325.

[20] Moultrie, *Memoirs*, 1: 328-41.

[21] Moultrie, *Memoirs*, 1: 353.

[22] Heidler, "The American Defeat at Briar Creek," 330; Wilson, *The Southern Strategy*, 96; Howard, "'Things here wear a melancholy appearance,'" 494.

[23] Moultrie, *Memoirs*, 1: 324-25.

[24] K.G. Davies, *Documents of the American Revolution, 1770-178* (Shannon: Irish University Press, 1972), 17: 78.

Notes to Chapter 4:
Afterword

[1] William Moultrie, *Memoirs of the American Revolution*, (New York: The New York Times & Arno Press, 1968), 1: 326.

[2] Joshua B. Howard, "'Things here wear a melancholy appearance:' The American Defeat at Briar Creek," *Georgia Historical Quarterly* 88.4 (Winter 2004), 498; David K. Wilson, *The Southern Strategy: Britain's Conquest of South Carolina and Georgia, 1775-1780* (Columbia: University of South Carolina Press, 2005), 90.

[3] Archibald Campbell, *Journal of an Expedition against the Rebels of Georgia in North America under the Orders of Archibald Campbell Esquire Lieut. Colol. of His Majesty's 71st Regimt. 1778*, ed. Colin Campbell (Augusta, Georgia: Richmond County Historical Society, 1981), 78.

[4] Campbell, *Journal of an Expedition*, 79-80.

[5] Campbell, *Journal of an Expedition*, 79.

[6] K.G. Davies, *Documents of the American Revolution, 1770-178* (Shannon: Irish University Press, 1972), 17:143.

[7] Campbell, *Journal of an Expedition*, 81.

[8] Campbell, *Journal of an Expedition*, x.

[9] John C. Dann, *The Revolution Remembered: Eyewitness accounts of the War for Independence* (Chicago: University of Chicago Press, 1980), 177.

[10] Dann, *The Revolution Remembered*, 181.

[11] Dann, *The Revolution Remembered*, 181-84.

[12] Dann, *The Revolution Remembered*, 185.

[13] Dann, *The Revolution Remembered*, 177.

[14] John McKay Sheftall, *Sunbury on the Medway: A Selective History of the Town, Inhabitants and Fortifications* (Atlanta: State of Georgia Department of

Natural Resources Office of Planning and Research, Historic Preservation Section, 1977), 47-52, 135.

[15] Dann, *The Revolution Remembered*, 179-80.

Notes to Chapter 5:
An Accusation of Atrocities

[1] Henry Onderdonk, *Revolutionary Incidents of Suffolk and Kings Counties: with an account of the Battle of Long Island and the British prisons and prison-ships at New York* (New York: Leavitt, 1849), 138.

[2] William E. Cox, "Brigadier-General John Ashe's Defeat in the Battle of Brier Creek," *Georgia Historical Quarterly* 57.2 (Summer 1973), 302.

[3] Alexander A. Lawrence, "General Robert Howe and the British Capture of Savannah in 1778," *Georgia Historical Quarterly* 36.4 (1952): 307.

[4] Colin Campbell, ed., *Journal of an Expedition against the Rebels of Georgia in North America under the Orders of Archibald Campbell Esquire Lieut. Colol. of His Majesty's 71st Regimt. 1778*, ed. Colin Campbell (Augusta, Georgia: Richmond County Historical Society, 1981), 105.

[5] "Narrative of Mordecai Sheftall," *Setting Out to Begin a New World: Colonial Georgia, A Documentary History,* ed. Edward J. Cashin (Savannah: Beehive Press, 1995), 182-183.

[6] Elizabeth Lichtenstein Johnston, *Recollections of a Georgia Loyalist,* (Spartanburg: The Reprint Company, 1974), 48-49.

[7] Lawrence, "General Robert Howe," 323-24.

[8] Colin Campbell, *Journal of an Expedition,* 110.

[9] Lawrence, "General Robert Howe," 323.

[10] Colin Campbell, *Journal of an Expedition*, 77; K.G. Davies, *Documents of the American Revolution, 1770-178* (Shannon: Irish University Press, 1972), 17: 78.

[11] Colin Campbell, *Journal of an Expedition*, 105; Howard, 498.

[12] Quoted in Cox, "Brigadier-General John Ashe's Defeat," 299-300.

Notes to Chapter 6:
Legendary Last-second Rescues

[1] Frances Letcher Mitchell, *Georgia Land and People* (Spartanburg, S.C.: The Reprint Company, 1974), 75.

[2] Wm. Berrien Burroughs, "Samuel Elbert," in *Men of Mark of Georgia, Vol. 1*, Ed. William J. Northen (Atlanta: A.B. Caldwell, 1907), 60-61.

[3] "General Samuel Elbert," marker erected by the Grand Lodge of Georgia Free and Accepted Masons in Screven County on Brannens Bridge Road at Brier Creek, 11 miles NE of Sylvania.

[4] David S. Heidler, "The American defeat at Briar Creek, 3 March 1779," *Georgia Historical Quarterly* 66.3 (Fall 1982), 329-30.

Notes to Chapter 7:
The Legend of Cannon Lake

[1] Lamar Zipperer, "Information Regarding the Historical Significance of Tuckahoe and Cannon Lake," (Sylvania, Georgia: University of Georgia Extension Service, 1999), 1.

[2] William Moultrie, *Memoirs of the American Revolution*, (New York: The New York Times & Arno Press, 1968), 1:317-18.

[3] Otis Ashmore and Charles H. Olmstead, "Battles of Kettle Creek and Brier Creek" *Georgia Historical Quarterly* 10 (June 1926), 101.

Notes to Chapter 8:
The Adventures of John McIntosh

[1] George White, *Historical Collections of Georgia* (Baltimore: Genealogical Publishing Company, 1969), 470-74.

[2] Patrick Murray, "Memoir of Major Patrick Murray, Who Served in the 60th from 1770 to 1793," in *The Annals of the King's Royal Rifle Corps, Vol. 1: The Royal Americans,* ed. Lewis Butler (London: Smith, Elder & Co., 1913), 310-11.

[3] Gordon Burns Smith, *Morningstars of Liberty: The Revolutionary War in Georgia 1775-1783* (Milledgeville, Georgia: Boyd Publishing, 2006), 2:170.

[4] R.J. Massey, "John McIntosh," in *Men in Georgia,* ed. William J. Northen, (Atlanta: A.B. Caldwell, 1907), 242.

[5] Massey, "John McIntosh," 243.

[6] Smith, *Morningstars,* 2: 170.

[7] Massey, "John McIntosh," 243; Mark M. Boatner III, *Encyclopedia of the American Revolution* (New York: David McKay Company, 1976), 692; Lilla M. Hawes, ed., "The Papers of James Jackson 1781-1798," *Collections of the Georgia Historical Society Vol. XI* (Savannah: Georgia Historical Society, 1935), 19.

[8] Smith, *Morningstars,* 2: 170.

[9] White, *Historical Collections of Georgia,* 547-48.

[10] Smith, *Morningstars,* 2: 170.

[11] White, *Historical Collections of Georgia,* 549.

[12] Margaret Cate Davis, *Our Todays and Yesterdays* (Brunswick, Georgia: Glover Bros. Inc., 1930), 188-89. Page 170 of volume two of *Morningstars of Liberty*

by Gordon Burns Smith, McIntosh married the widow of William Stevens in September of 1799 in Liberty County.

[13] Gordon Burns Smith, *History of the Georgia Militia, Vol. 1: Campaigns and Generals* (Milledgeville, Georgia: Boyd Publishing, 2000), 388.

[14] Smith, *History of the Georgia Militia, Vol. 1*, 148; "John McIntosh," GlynnGen.com.

[15] White, *Historical Collections of Georgia,* 548-50; "John McIntosh," Glynn Gen.com; Smith, *History of the Georgia Militia, Vol. 1*, 322.

[16] Buddy Sullivan, *Early Days on the Georgia Tidewater: The Story of McIntosh County & Sapelo* (Darien: McIntosh County Board of Commissioners, 1990), 35-36.

[17] "Colonel John McIntosh laid to rest for the third time in McIntosh Co.," *The Darien News* (28 Oct. 2010), 1.

[18] Smith, *Morningstars*, 2: 171.

Notes to Chapter 9:
Bodies in Motion

[1] Elizabeth Carpenter Piechocinski, *The Old Burying Ground: Colonial Park Cemetery, Savannah, Georgia 1750-1853* (Savannah: The Oglethorpe Press, 1999), 30-34.

[2] "Colonel John McIntosh laid to rest for the third time in McIntosh Co.," *The Darien News* (28 Oct. 2010), 17, 19.

[3] "Colonel John McIntosh laid to rest," 17.

Notes to Chapter 10:
Reflections of Legends

[1] Joseph Campbell, *The Hero with a Thousand Faces* (Princeton: Princeton University Press, 1973), 238.

[2] Joseph Campbell with Bill Moyers, *The Power of Myth* (New York: Doubleday, 1988), 114.

[3] John C. Dann, *The Revolution Remembered: Eyewitness accounts of the War for Independence* (Chicago: University of Chicago Press, 1980), 181.

[4] Northrop Frye, *The secular scripture: A study of the structure of romance* (Cambridge, Mass.: Harvard University Press, 1976), 136.

[5] Joseph Campbell, *The Masks of God: Creative Mythology* (New York: Penguin, 1991), 558.

[6] Campbell, *The Masks of God: Creative Mythology*, 559.

[7] Campbell, *The Masks of God: Creative Mythology,* 470.

[8] (*Celtic Mythology (*New Lanark, Scotland: Geddes & Gosset, 1999), 413.

[9] Corinne Saunders, "Religion and Magic," in *The Cambridge Guide to the Arthurian Legend,* ed. Elizabeth Archibald and Ad Putter (Cambridge: Cambridge University Press, 2009), 210.

[10] Jean Chevalier and Alain Gheerbrant, *The Penguin Dictionary of Symbols* (New York: Penguin Books, 1996), 808; Michael Ferber, *A Dictionary of Literary Symbols* (Cambridge: Cambridge University Press, 2007), 170.

[11] Robert Allen Rouse and Cory James Rushton, "Arthurian Geography," in *The Cambridge Guide to the Arthurian Legend,* ed. Elizabeth Archibald and Ad Putter (Cambridge: Cambridge University Press, 2009), 222.

[12] Saunders, "Religion and Magic," 212.

[13] Campbell, *The Masks of God: Creative Mythology,* 474-75, 476.

[14] Peter Berresford Ellis, *A Dictionary of Irish Mythology* (Oxford: Oxford University Press, 1991), 85, 220.

[15] Rouse and Rushton, "Arthurian Geography," 223.

Notes to Chapter 11: Samuel Elbert

[1] Clay Ouzts, "'A Good Bargain for the Trust:' The Ordeal of William and Sarah Elbert, 1733-1742," *Georgia Historical Quarterly* 101.1 (2017): 28, 30, 33.

[2] Ouzts, "A Good Bargain," 33, 36, 39, 43, 45.

[3] Ouzts, "A Good Bargain," 45, 46, 47.

[4] Charles C. Jones, Jr., *The Life andSservice of the Honorable Major General Samuel Elbert of Georgia*, 1887 (Charleston, S.C.: BiblioLife, 2011), 8; Elizabeth Carpenter Piechocinski, *The Old Burying Ground: Colonial Park Cemetery, Savannah, Georgia 1750-1853* (Savannah: The Oglethorpe Press, 1999), 31; Beryl I. Diamond, "Samuel Elbert (1740-1788)," New Georgia Encyclopedia, <http://www.georgiaencyclopedia.org/search/ advanced/samuel%20elbert> (accessed August 22, 2017); Gordon Burns Smith, *Morningstars of Liberty* (Milledgeville, Georgia: Boyd Publishing, 2011), 2: 111-12.

[5] Diamond, "Samuel Elbert," Web.

[6] Gordon Burns Smith, *Morningstars of Liberty: The Revolutionary War in Georgia 1775-1783* (Milledgeville, Georgia: Boyd Publishing, 2006), 2:19.

[7] Harvey Hardaway Jackson III, *Lachlan McIntosh and the Politics of Revolutionary Georgia*, 1979 (Athens: University of Georgia Press, 2003), 29-33; Smith, *Morningstars*, 2:19.

[8] Martha Condray Searcy, *The Georgia-Florida Contest in the American Revolution, 1776-1778* (University, Ala.: University of Alabama Press, 1985), 54-62.

[9] Searcy, *The Georgia-Florida Contest*, 79, 88-90; Alexander A. Lawrence, "General Lachlan McIntosh and His Suspension from Continental Command During the Revolution," *Georgia Historical Quarterly* 38 no. 2 (1954), 111; Jackson, *Lachlan McIntosh*, 54-55.

[10] Lachlan McIntosh to Samuel Elbert, Headquarters, January 8, 1777, *Papers of Lachlan McIntosh, 1774-1779*, ed. Lilla M. Hawes (Savannah: Georgia Historical Society, 1957), 34.

[11] Lachlan McIntosh to George Wells, Savannah, July 14, 1777, quoted in Charles Francis Jenkins, *Button Gwinnett: Signer of the Declaration of Independence* (New York: Doubleday, Page & Company, 1926), 259.

[12] Lawrence, "Suspension," 113-14.

[13] "Order Book of Samuel Elliott, Colonel and Brigadier General in the Continental Army, October 1776 to November 1778," *Collections of the Georgia Historical Society Vol. V, Part 2* (Savannah: The Morning News Print, 1902), 19.

[14] Lachlan McIntosh to George Wells, Savannah, July 14, 1777, quoted in Jenkins, *Button Gwinnett*, 259.

[15] Lachlan McIntosh to Samuel Elbert, Savannah, April 26, 1777, *Papers of Lachlan McIntosh*, 48.

[16] Searcy, *Georgia-Florida Contest*, 92-94.

[17] Searcy, *Georgia-Florida Contest*, 94.

[18] Searcy, *Georgia-Florida Contest*, 95.

[19] "Order Book of Samuel Elliott," 33.

[20] "Order Book of Samuel Elliott," 35.

[21] "Order Book of Samuel Elliott," 33.

[22] "Order Book of Samuel Elliott," 33.

[23] Searcy, *Georgia-Florida Contest*, 93-96.

[24] Searcy, *Georgia-Florida Contest*, 95-97.

[25] "Order Book of Samuel Elliott," 37.

[26] "Order Book of Samuel Elliott," 46.

[27] Jenkins, *Button Gwinnett*, 229.

[28] "George Wells' Affidavit respecting B.G. and L.M. June 1777," quoted in Edward G. Williams, ed. "A Revolutionary Journal and Orderly Book of General Lachlan McIntosh's Expedition, 1778," *The Western Pennsylvania Historical Magazine* 43 (1960): 3.

[29] "George Wells' Affidavit," 3.

[30] Kenneth Coleman, *The American Revolution in Georgia* (Athens: University of Georgia Press, 1958), 87-89; E. Merton Coulter, *Georgia: A Short History*, 3rd ed. (Chapel Hill: University of North Carolina Press, 1960), 134-35; Jackson, *Lachlan McIntosh*, 64-66; Lachlan McIntosh to Henry Laurens, Savannah, May 30, 1777, P.S., June 3, 1777, quoted in Jenkins, *Button Gwinnett*, 255.

[31] "Order Book of Samuel Elliott," 1902), 49-50.

[32] "Order Book of Samuel Elliott," 52.

[33] "Order Book of Samuel Elliott," 55.

[34] Order Book of Samuel Elliott," 56.

[35] "Order Book of Samuel Elliott," 61.

[36] Coleman, *The American Revolution in Georgia*, 107; Coulter, *Georgia: A Short History*, 135-36; Searcy, *Georgia-Florida Contest*, 134).

[37] "Order Book of Samuel Elliott," 128.

[38] Samuel Elbert to Robert Howe, Frederica, April 19, 1778, quoted in Wm. Berrien Burroughs, "Samuel Elbert," in *Men of Mark in Georgia* (Atlanta: A.B. Caldwell, 1907), 1: 59-60.

[39] Searcy, *Georgia-Florida Contest*, 134-35; Smith, *Morningstars*, 1:104-05.

[40] "Order Book of Samuel Elliott," 128.

[41] Coulter, *Georgia: A Short History*, 136; Searcy, *Georgia-Florida Contest*, 136, 139).

[42] "Order Book of Samuel Elliott," 142.

[43] "Order Book of Samuel Elliott," 149.

[44] Searcy, *Georgia-Florida Contest*, 140, 142.

[45] Searcy, *Georgia-Florida Contest*, 144-45.

[46] Searcy, *Georgia-Florida Contest*, 145.

[47] "Order Book of Samuel Elliott," 177.

[48] "Order Book of Samuel Elliott," 178.

[49] "Order Book of Samuel Elliott," 183.

[50] "Order Book of Samuel Elliott," 187-88.

[51] "Order Book of Samuel Elliott," 188.

[52] Searcy, *Georgia-Florida Contest*, 179-80).

[53] R.J. Massey, "John McIntosh," in *Men of Mark in Georgia* (Atlanta: A.B. Caldwell, 1907), 1: 241-42.

[54] Wm. Berrien Burroughs, "Samuel Elbert," in *Men of Mark in Georgia* (Atlanta: A.B. Caldwell, 1907), 1: 61; Smith, *Morningstars*, 2: 112.

[55] James F. Cook, *The Governors of Georgia 1754-2004* (Macon, Georgia: Mercer University Press, 2005), 56.

[56] Jones, *Samuel Elbert*, 28.

[57] Burroughs, "Samuel Elbert," 61.

[58] Cook, *Governors of Georgia*, 57.

[59] "Letter Book of Governor Samuel Elliott, from January, 1785, to November 1785," *Collections of the Georgia Historical Society* Vol. V, Part 2 (Savannah: The Morning News Print, 1902), 195.

[60] "Letter Book of Governor Samuel Elliott," 204.

[61] "Letter Book of Governor Samuel Elliott," 204.

[62] "Letter Book of Governor Samuel Elliott," 197.

[63] "Letter Book of Governor Samuel Elliott," 196.

[64] Cook, *Governors of Georgia*, 56-57; Jones, *Samuel Elbert*, 30.

[65] Quoted in Jones, *Samuel Elbert*, 31-32.

Notes to Chapter 12: Remember Brier Creek

[1] "Editor's Notes," *Georgia Historical Quarterly* 1:2 (1917), 170.

[2] Cypress Creek Consultants, "Locating the Forgotten Revolutionary War Battle of Brier Creek (9SN254); Metal Detector Survey, Burial Search, and Extensive Archival Research" (Sylvania, Georgia: City of Sylvania, 2014), 164-70; personal communication with Dawn Daley of the DAR, Jan. 2, 2017.

[3] Enoch Autry, "Sons of American Revolution chapter now at Brier Creek," *The Sylvania Telephone* 24 Nov. 2016, 1,9; Daniel Battle, "The Continuing Battle of Brier Creek," *The Hornet's Nest* (April-June 2016), 31.

[4] "Registrar's Report," *Brier Creek Patriot* (Jan. 2018), 2.

[5] Enoch Autry, "UGA faculty and student group details plan, memorial for Battle of Brier Creek," *The Sylvania Telephone* 19 Nov. 2015, 1, 6-7.

[6] Enoch Autry, "A battle of importance," *The Sylvania Telephone* 3 March 2016, 8.

[7] Autry, "A battle of importance," 8; Enoch Autry, "Battle of Brier Creek memorial takes another step toward reality: 237 years in the making," *The Sylvania Telephone* 10 Nov. 2016, 10.

[8] "Lee honored for his outstanding archives." *The Sylvania Telephone* 3 Nov. 2016, 1, 8.

[9] Enoch Autry, "Battle of Brier Creek progresses," *The Sylvania Telephone*, 2 March 2017, 1.

[10] Enoch Autry, "Battle memorial funding of historical value," *The Sylvania Telephone*, 2 March 2017, 1.

[11] Author's notes, Sylvania, Georgia, 18 July 2017.

Notes to Chapter 13:
Come See Us

[1] Dan Johnson, "Battle site rarely gets recognition," *The Sylvania Telephone* 9 Aug. 1996, 1.

Notes to Chapter 14:
The Brier Creek Battleground

[1] "Brier Creek Commemorative Conceptual Masterplan," Georgia Department of Natural Resources and Wildlife Resources Division, September 21, 2016.

[2] Enoch Autry, "Memorializing our Patriots," *The Sylvania Telephone*, 8 March 2018, 8.

[3] Autry, "Memorializing our Patriots," 8.

[4] Enoch Autry, "Historic signing of Brier Creek Association by-laws," *The Sylvania Telephone*, 19 April 2018, 5.

[5] "Summary of Proposed National Register/Georgia Register Nomination," Georgia National Register Review Board, December 2017. <http://georgiashpo.org/up comingreviewboard> (accessed Feb. 22, 2018).

Notes to Chapter 16:
Along the Savannah River

[1] Archibald Campbell, *Journal of an Expedition against the Rebels of Georgia in North America under the Orders of Archibald Campbell Esquire Lieut. Colol. of His Majesty's 71st Regimt. 1778*, ed. Colin Campbell (Augusta, Georgia: Richmond County Historical Society, 1981), 41.

[2] Campbell, *Journal of an Expedition*, 29-30.

[3] "Points of Interest," Jasper County Chamber of Commerce, <http://www.jaspercountychamber.com/discover_jasper_county/point_of_interest.htm> (accessed Dec. 5, 2016).

[4] Campbell, *Journal of an Expedition*, 42.

[5] Campbell, *Journal of an Expedition*, 46.

[6] Robert Scott Davis Jr., *Encounters on a March Through Georgia in 1779: The Maps and Memorandums of John Wilson, Engineer, 71st Highland Regiment* (Sylvania, Georgia: Partridge Pond Press, 1986), 55, n. 68.

[7] Davis, *Encounters*, 23, 25.

[8] Campbell, *Journal of an Expedition*, 42.

[9] Davis, *Encounters*, 25, 27.

[10] Davis, *Encounters*, 49, n. 24.

[11] Author's recollection, near Newington, Georgia, 21 Feb. 2016; "Corps of Discovery," *Southern Campaigns of the American Revolution*. <http://www.southerncampaign.org/> (accessed July 26, 2018).

[12] Davis, *Encounters*, 58, n. 92.

[13] Davis, *Encounters*, 27, 29.

[14] Davis, *Encounters*, 29.

[15] Campbell, *Journal of an Expedition*, 68.

[16] Davis, *Encounters*, 58, n. 96; Robert S. Davis, "Civil War in the Midst of Revolution: Community Divisions and the Battle of Briar Creek, 1779," *Georgia Historical Quarterly* 100.2 (Summer 2016), 144.

[17] Davis, *Encounters*, 29, 31.

[18] Campbell, *Journal of an Expedition*, 27.

[19] Alexania Easterling Lawton and Minnie Reeves Wilson, *Allendale on the Savannah* (Bamberg, S.C.: Bamberg Herald Printers, 1970), 10.

[20] James Kilgo, *Pipe Creek to Matthews Bluff: A short history of Groton Plantation* (Chelsea, Mich.: Book Crafters, 1994), 16-18.

[21] Lawton and Wilson, *Allendale on the Savannah*, 25.

[22] Kilgo, *Pipe Creek to Matthews Bluff,* 22; Joshua B. Howard, "'Things here wear a melancholy appearance:' The American Defeat at Briar Creek," *Georgia Historical Quarterly* 88.4 (Winter 2004), 488-96; Arthur Gross, "Battle of Brier Creek Was Fought 200 Years Ago," *The Sylvania Telephone,* 1 Mar. 1979, 9.

[23] Lawton and Wilson, *Allendale on the Savannah,* 23.

[24] Lawton and Wilson, *Allendale on the Savannah,* 22-23; "South Carolina Revolutionary Battles," *Names in South Carolina* 30 (Winter 1983), 10.

[25] Lawton and Wilson, *Allendale on the Savannah,* 2.

[26] Lawton and Wilson, *Allendale on the Savannah,* 15.

[27] Lawton and Wilson, *Allendale on the Savannah,* 2, 9, 15-16; Thomas L. Stokes, *The Savannah* (Athens, Georgia: University of Georgia Press, 1982), 11-12.

[28] Lawton and Wilson, *Allendale on the Savannah,* 2-3; Ethel. Rouse, "Story of Western Allendale County Centering on Barton" in *Allendale on the Savannah* by Alexania Easterling Lawton and Minnie Reeves Wilson (Bamberg, S.C.: Bamberg Herald Printers, 1970), 394.

[29] Davis, *Encounters*, 59, n. 98

[30] Campbell, *Journal of an Expedition,* 56.

[31] *Augusta, Georgia,* <https://www.visitaugusta.com/listing/saint-pauls-episcopal-church/5/> (accessed 5 Dec. 5, 2016).

[32] Campbell, *Journal of an Expedition,* 54-55.

[33] Davis, *Encounters,* 37.

Bibliography

American Revolution Roster: Fort Sullivan (later Fort Moultrie), 1776-1780. Charleston, S.C.: Fort Sullivan Chapter of the Daughters of the American Revolution, 1976.

Ashmore, Otis and Charles H. Olmstead. "Battles of Kettle Creek and Brier Creek." *Georgia Historical Quarterly* 10 (June 1926): 85-125.

Autry, Enoch. "A battle of importance." *The Sylvania Telephone* 3 March 2016: 1, 8.

---. "Battle memorial funding of historical value." *The Sylvania Telephone* 2 March 2017: 1.

---. "Battle of Brier Creek memorial takes another step toward reality: 237 years in the making." *The Sylvania Telephone* 10 Nov. 2016: 1, 10.

---. "Battle of Brier Creek progresses." *The Sylvania Telephone* 2 March 2017: 1.

---. "Historic signing of Brier Creek Association by-laws." *The Sylvania Telephone*, 19 April 2018, 5.

---. "Memorializing our Patriots." *The Sylvania Telephone* 8 March 2018: 1, 8 ,9.

---. "Sons of American Revolution chapter now at Brier Creek." *The Sylvania Telephone* 24 Nov. 2016: 1, 9.

---. "UGA faculty and student group details plan, memorial for Battle of Brier Creek." *The Sylvania Telephone* 19 Nov. 2015: 1, 6-7.

Babits, Lawrence E. and Joshua B. Howard. *Long, obstinate and bloody: The Battle of Guilford Courthouse.* Chapel Hill: University of North Carolina Press, 2009.

Battle, Daniel. "The Continuing Battle of Brier Creek." *The Hornet's Nest* April-June 2016: 31.

Boatner III, Mark M. *Encyclopedia of the American Revolution*. New York: David McKay Company, 1976.

Borick, Carl P. *A Gallant Defense: The Siege of Charleston, 1780*. Columbia: University of South Carolina Press, 2003.

Burroughs, Wm. Berrien. "Samuel Elbert." *Men of Mark of Georgia Vol. I*. Ed. William J. Northen. Atlanta: A.B. Caldwell, 1907. 58-62.

Campbell, Colin, ed. *Journal of an expedition against the rebels of Georgia in North America under the orders of Archibald Campbell Esquire Lieut. Colol. of His Majesty's 71st Regimt. 1778*. Augusta, Georgia: Richmond County Historical Society, 1981.

Campbell, Joseph. *The Masks of God: Creative Mythology*. 1968. New York: Penguin, 1991.

---. *The Hero with a Thousand Faces*. 1949. Princeton: Princeton University Press, 1973.

--- with Bill Moyers. *The Power of Myth*. New York: Doubleday, 1988.

Cashin Jr., Edward J., and Heard Robertson. *Augusta and the American Revolution: Events in the Georgia Back Country, 1773-1783*. Augusta, Georgia: Richmond County Historical Society, 1975.

Cate, Margaret Davis. *Our Todays and Yesterdays: A Story of Brunswick and the Coastal Islands*. Spartanburg, South Carolina: The Reprint Company, 1972.

Celtic Mythology. New Lanark, Scotland: Geddes & Gosset, 1999.

Chevalier, Jean and Alain Gheerbrant. *The Penguin Dictionary of Symbols*. New York: Penguin Books, 1996.

"Colonel John McIntosh laid to rest for the third time in McIntosh Co." *The Darien News*, 28 Oct. 2010: 1+

Cook, James F. *The Governors of Georgia 1754-2004*. Macon, Georgia: Mercer University Press, 2005.

Cox, William E. "Brigadier-General John Ashe's Defeat in the Battle of Brier Creek." *Georgia Historical Quarterly* 57.2 (Summer 1973): 295-302.

Cypress Creek Consultants, "Locating the Forgotten Revolutionary War Battle of Brier Creek (9SN254); Metal Detector Survey, Burial Search, and Extensive Archival Research." Sylvania, Georgia: City of Sylvania, 2014.

Dann, John C. *The Revolution Remembered: Eyewitness accounts of the War for Independence*. Chicago: University of Chicago Press, 1980.

Davies, K.G. *Documents of the American Revolution, 1770-1783. Vol. 17*. Shannon: Irish University Press, 1972.

Davis Jr., Robert Scott. *Encounters on a March Through Georgia in 1779: The Maps and Memorandums of John Wilson, Engineer, 71st Highland Regiment*. Sylvania, Georgia: Partridge Pond Press, 1986.

---. *Georgians in the Revolution: At Kettle Creek (Wilkes County) and Burke County*. Easley, S.C.: Southern Historical Press, 1996.

---. "Civil War in the Midst of Revolution: Community Divisions and the Battle of Brier Creek, 1779." *Georgia Historical Quarterly* 100.2 (Summer 2016): 136-59.

Diamond, Beryl I. "Samuel Elbert (1740-1788)." *New Georgia Enclyclopedia*. 17 September 2014. <www.georgiaencyclopedia.org> Accessed 17 August 2017.

"Editor's Notes." *Georgia Historical Quarterly* 1.2 (June, 1917): 168-170.

Ellis, Peter Berresford. *A Dictionary of Irish Mythology*. Oxford: Oxford University Press, 1991.

Ferber, Michael. *A Dictionary of Literary Symbols*. Cambridge: Cambridge University Press, 2007.

Frye, Northrop. *The secular scripture: A study of the structure of romance*. Cambridge, Mass.: Harvard University Press, 1976.

"General John Ashe of North Carolina to Governor Caswell of North Carolina, March 17, 1779." *North Carolina State Records, XIV*, 39-43. Rpt. in *The Spirit of 'Seventy-Six*, Henry Steele Commager and Richard B. Morris. New York: Harper and Row, 1967. 1082-85.

"General Samuel Elbert." Marker erected by the Grand Lodge of Georgia Free and Accepted Masons in Screven County on Brannens Bridge Road at Brier Creek, 11 miles NE of Sylvania.

Gordon, William. *The history of the rise, progress, and establishment, of the independence of the United States of America: including an account of the late war*, Vol. 3. London, printed for the author, 1788. 4 vols. Sabin Americana. Gale, Cengage Learning. University of South Carolina. 20 July 2018 <<http://galenet.galegroup.com/servlet/Sabin?af=RN&ae=CY104349274&srchtp=a&ste=14>>

Gross, Arthur. "Battle of Brier Creek Was Fought 200 Years Ago." *The Sylvania Telephone,* 1 Mar. 1979, 9-10.

Hawes, Lilla M., ed. "The Papers of James Jackson 1781-1798." *Collections of the Georgia Historical Society Vol. XI*. Savannah: Georgia Historical Society, 1935.

Heidler, David S. "The American defeat at Briar Creek, 3 March 1779." *Georgia Historical Quarterly* 66.3 (Fall 1982): 317-31.

Howard, Joshua B., " 'Things here wear a melancholy appearance:' The American Defeat at Briar Creek." *Georgia Historical Quarterly* 88.4 (Winter 2004): 477-98.

Hunter, James. *A Dance Called America: The Scottish Highlands in the United States and Canada*. Edinburgh: Mainstream Publishing, 1994.

Jackson III, Harvey Hardaway. *Lachlan McIntosh and the Politics of Revolutionary Georgia.* 1979. Athens: University of Georgia Press, 2003.

"John McIntosh." *GlynnGen.com Coastal Georgia Genealogy & History.* <http://www.glynn gen.com/military/amrev/ glynn/mcintoshjno.htm> Accessed 10 March 2011.

Johnson, Dan. "Battle site rarely gets recognition." *The Sylvania Telephone* 9 Aug. 1996: 1-2.

Johnston, Elizabeth Lichtenstein. *Recollections of a Georgia Loyalist.* 1836. Spartanburg: The Reprint Company, 1974.

Jones Jr., Charles C. *The History of Georgia.* 1883. Spartanburg, S.C.: The Reprint Company, 1969.

---. *The life and service of the honorable Major General Samuel Elbert of Georgia.* 1887. Charleston, S.C.: BiblioLife, 2011.

Kilgo, James. *Pipe Creek to Matthews Bluff: A short history of Groton Plantation.* Chelsea, Mich.: Book Crafters, c. 1994.

Lanier, Sidney. *Florida: Its Scenery, Climate, and History. A facsimile reproduction of the 1875 edition with introduction and index by Jerrell H. Shofner.* Gainesville: University of Florida Press, 1973.

Lawrence, Alexander A. "General Robert Howe and the British Capture of Savannah in 1778." *Georgia Historical Quarterly* 36.4 (1952): 303-327.

Lawton, Alexania Easterling and Minnie Reeves Wilson. *Allendale on the Savannah.* Bamberg, S.C.: Bamberg Herald Printers, 1970.

Lee, Rabun A. [Alex]. Personal communication. July-August 1996. He conducted a tour of the Brier Creek battleground and also provided photocopies of his research. Lee is a local historian from Sylvania, Georgia, who has written about the Battle of Brier Creek for a brochure published by Georgia Society Sons of the American Revolution.

"Lee honored for his outstanding archives." *The Sylvania Telephone* 3 Nov. 2016: 1, 8.

"Letter Book of Governor Samuel Elliott, from January,1785, to November 1785." *Collections of the Georgia Historical Society Vol. V, Part 2.* Savannah: The Morning News Print, 1902. 193-223.

Lewis, Bessie. *They Called Their Town Darien.* Darien, Georgia: The Darien News, 1975.

Lumpkin, Henry. *From Savannah to Yorktown: The American Revolution in the South.* Columbia: University of South Carolina Press, 1981.

Macinlay, James M. *Folklore of Scottish Lochs and Springs.* 1893. Felinfach, Wales: Llanerch Publishers, 1993

Mackintosh of Mackintosh, Margaret, revised by Lachlan Mackintosh of Mackintosh, 30th Chief of Mackintosh. *The History of Clan Mackintosh and Clan Chattan.* Edinburgh: The Pentland Press Limited, 1997.

Martin, Bobby M. *Wayne County, Georgia: Its history and its people.* Dallas: Curtis Media Corp., 1990.

Massey, R.J. "John McIntosh." *Men of Mark of Georgia Vol. I.* Ed. William J. Northen. Atlanta: A.B. Caldwell, 1907. 241-45.

McIlvaine, Paul. *The Dead Town of Sunbury, Georgia.* Hendersonville, N.C.: Paul M. McIlvaine, 1971.

Mitchell, Frances Letcher. *Georgia Land and People.* 1900. Spartanburg, S.C.: The Reprint Company, 1974.

Moore, Frank. *Diary of the American Revolution from Newspapers and Original Documents Vol. 2.* 1860. New York: The New York Times & Arno Press, 1969.

Moultrie, William. *Memoirs of the American Revolution.* 1802. New York: The New York Times & Arno Press, 1968.

Murray, Patrick. "Memoir of Major Patrick Murray, Who Served in the 60th from 1770 to 1793." *The Annals of the King's Royal Rifle Corps. Volume 1: The Royal Americans.* Lewis Butler, ed. (London: Smith, Elder & Co., 1913. 288-319.

"Narrative of Mordecai Sheftall." *Setting Out to Begin a New World: Colonial Georgia, A Documentary History.* Ed. Edward J. Cashin. Savannah: Beehive Press, 1995. 182-85.

Onderdonk, Henry. *Revolutionary Incidents of Suffolk and Kings Counties: with an account of the Battle of Long Island and the British prisons and prison-ships at New York.* New York: Leavitt, 1849.

"Order Book of Samuel Elliott, Colonel and Brigadier General in the Continental Army, October 1776 to November 1778." *Collections of the Georgia Historical Society Vol. V, Part 2.* Savannah: The Morning News Print, 1902. 5-191.

Ouzts, Clay. " 'A Good Bargain for the Trust:' The Ordeal of William and Sarah Elbert, 1733-1742." *Georgia Historical Quarterly* 101.1 (2017): 25-52.

Piechocinski, Elizabeth Carpenter. *The Old Burying Ground: Colonial Park Cemetery, Savannah, Georgia 1750-1853.* Savannah: The Oglethorpe Press, 1999.

"Registrar's Report." *Brier Creek Patriot* 3.1 (January, 2018): 2.

Robertson, R. Macdonald. *Selected Highland Folktales.* Nairn, Scotland: David St John Thomas Publisher, 1993

Ross, Anne, *The Folklore of the Scottish Highlands.* London: B.T. Batsford Ltd., 1976.

Rouse, Ethel. "Story of Western Allendale County Centering on Barton." *Allendale on the Savannah.* Alexania Easterling Lawton and Minnie Reeves Wilson. Bamberg, S.C.: Bamberg Herald Printers, 1970.

Rouse, Robert Allen and Cory James Rushton. "Arthurian geography." *The Cambridge Guide to the Arthurian Legend.* Ed. Elizabeth Archibald and Ad Putter. Cambridge: Cambridge University Press, 2009. 218-234.

Saunders, Corinne. "Religion and Magic." *The Cambridge Guide to the Arthurian Legend.* Ed. Elizabeth Archibald and Ad Putter. Cambridge: Cambridge University Press, 2009. 201-217.

Sheftall, John McKay. *Sunbury on the Medway: A Selective History of the Town, Inhabitants and Fortifications.* Atlanta: State of Georgia Department of Natural Resources Office of Planning and Research, Historic Preservation Section, 1977.

Smith, Gordon Burns. *Morningstars of Liberty: The Revolutionary War in Georgia 1775-1783.* 2 vols. Milledgeville, Georgia: Boyd Publishing, 2006.

---. *History of the Georgia Militia, Vol. 1: Campaigns and Generals.* Milledgeville, Georgia: Boyd Publishing, 2000.

"South Carolina Revolutionary Battles." *Names in South Carolina* 30 (Winter 1983), 10-16.

Stokes, Thomas L. *The Savannah.* 1951. Athens, Georgia: University of Georgia Press, 1982.

Sullivan, Buddy. *Early Days on the Georgia Tidewater: The Story of McIntosh County & Sapelo.* Darien: McIntosh County Board of Commissioners, 1990.

"Summary of Proposed National Register/Georgia Register Nomination." Georgia National Register Review Board, December 2017. <http://georgiashpo.org/upcomingreviewboard> Accessed 22 Feb. 2018.

White, George. *Historical Collections of Georgia.* 1855. Baltimore: Genealogical Publishing Company, 1969.

Wilson, David K. *The Southern Strategy: Britain's Conquest of South Carolina and Georgia, 1775-1780.* Columbia: University of South Carolina Press, 2005.

Zipperer, Lamar. "Information Regarding the Historical Significance of Tuckahoe and Cannon Lake." Sylvania, Georgia: University of Georgia Extension Service, 1999.

Index

Ashe, John, 17, 21, 23, 24, 25, 26, 27, 28, 29, 31, 36, 128, 129, 130, 144, 145, 158, 159
Augusta, 1, 3, 5, 6, 7, 3, 9, 12, 13, 14, 15, 16, 23, 31, 32, 51, 52, 56, 74, 81, 84, 85, 87, 88, 102, 122, 130, 134, 135, 136, 137, 139, 140, 142, 143, 144, 154, 156, 158
Baird, James, 22, 39, 40, 41, 43, 44
Battle, Daniel, 95
Brier Creek, 1, 2, 3, 5, 6, 7, 3, 13, 19, 21, 22, 23, 24, 25, 28, 29, 30, 31, 33, 36, 39, 43, 44, 47, 48, 51, 52, 56, 61, 65, 66, 67, 68, 69, 74, 86, 93, 94, 95, 99, 100, 101, 102, 103, 104, 105, 107, 108, 109, 110, 111, 112, 113, 115, 116, 119, 126, 127, 129, 133, 134, 135, 141, 144, 145, 146, 153, 154, 156, 157, 158, 159, 160, 161, 163
Brier Creek Revolutionary War Battlefield Association, 113
Burton's Ferry, 6, 21, 24, 116, 133
Campbell, Archibald, 5, 6, 7, 8, 10, 11, 12, 13, 14, 15, 16, 17, 18, 19, 26, 31, 32, 33, 43, 117, 118, 120, 121, 122, 123, 126, 127, 134, 135, 137, 139, 140, 142, 143, 144, 145, 148, 154, 155, 156, 158
Cannon Lake, 5, 51, 52, 67, 109, 126, 127, 145, 164
Cohens Bluff, 132, *See* Matthews Bluff
Daughters of the American Revolution, 94, 97, 111, 157
Ebenezer, 6, 18, 85, 120, 121, 122, 123
Elbert, Samuel, 3, 5, 8, 9, 10, 13, 14, 15, 16, 21,

22, 24, 25, 26, 27, 30,
35, 36, 47, 48, 61, 62,
63, 66, 73–89, 94, 108,
112, 113, 139, 145,
149, 150, 151, 152,
158, 159, 160, 161, 163
Evans, Margaret, 95, 111
Fergus, James, 23, 24, 26,
27, 28, 33, 34, 35, 36,
66
Freeland, A.L., 95, 113
Freeman-Miller Bridge.
See Miller Bridge
Georgia Department of
Natural Resources, 96,
97, 102, 107, 108, 110,
111, 116, 144, 154, 163
Howe, Robert, 5, 9, 10,
31, 80, 81, 82, 83, 84,
139, 144, 151, 161
Hudson's Ferry, 6, 17, 18,
24, 51, 125, 126
Lee, Alex, 39, 93, 94, 96,
97, 99
Lincoln, Benjamin, 14,
16, 32, 35, 119, 120,
122, 123
MacAlister, Hugh, 16, 26
Marbury, Leonard, 24
Matthews Bluff, 6, 22,
116, 128, 129, 130,
131, 132, 156, 161
McIntosh, Billy, 63, 64
McIntosh, John, 2, 5, 47,
53, 54, 55, 56, 58, 59,
61, 63, 64, 66, 86, 99,
146, 147, 149, 150,
151, 152, 158, 160,
162, 164
McIntosh, Lachlan, 55,
75, 76, 77, 80, 81
McIntosh, Roderick, 53,
54
Miller Bridge, 6, 21, 26,
126, 127, 128
Moultrie, William, 28,
29, 31, 52, 76, 141,
142, 143, 145, 157, 162
Paris's Mill, 18, 22, 23,
24, 103, 134
Prevost, Augustine, 12,
17, 18, 30, 32, 33, 34,
43
Prevost, James Mark, 17,
18, 19, 22, 25, 33, 78,
126
Purrysburg, 6, 16, 21, 23,
28, 32, 52, 73, 119,
122, 131
Remember Brier Creek
Committee, 94, 96, 97,
100, 111, 113
Ross, Francis, 23, 24,
131, 163
Savannah, 1, 3, 5, 6, 7, 3,
5, 9, 10, 12, 13, 17, 18,
19, 21, 31, 32, 35, 41,
42, 43, 59, 61, 62, 63,
73, 74, 75, 77, 79, 80,
84, 85, 86, 87, 101,
104, 105, 117, 118,
119, 133, 136, 139,

141, 144, 146, 147,
149, 150, 151, 152,
154, 155, 156, 160,
161, 162, 163, 164
Savannah River, 6, 5, 7,
8, 9, 13, 14, 15, 16, 19,
21, 22, 23, 25, 27, 28,
34, 52, 66, 67, 68, 73,
74, 75, 80, 87, 99, 100,
101, 102, 104, 105,
115, 116, 117, 119,
120, 121, 125, 128,
129, 131, 132, 133,
135, 136, 154

Seventy-first Regiment,
6, 7, 16, 22, 25, 35, 39,
42, 43, 122, 125
Sisters Ferry. *See* Two
Sisters Ferry
Sons of the American
Revolution, 95, 97,
101, 111, 112, 161
Stone, Jesse, 96, 97, 113
Sunbury, 12, 35, 53, 54,
55, 75, 77, 80, 83, 85,
86, 88, 143, 162, 163
Tuckasee King, 124
Two Sisters Ferry, 123
Wiggins Hill, 130

www.ingramcontent.com/pod-product-compliance
Lightning Source LLC
Chambersburg PA
CBHW051947290426
44110CB00015B/2150